Weedmonkey

Mama, Mother, Whore

Lisa V. Proulx

Cover design by Lisa V. Proulx

Photo is from author's personal collection.

ISBN: 1490912924
ISBN-13: 978-1490912929

For my mother Victoria

CHAPTERS

Acknowledgements

To Steve, thank you for your love, encouragement and support. You are the wind beneath my wings. ♥

To my wonderful editor, Susan Hughes, who made this book shine: There is no one else in the world I would have trusted with *Weedmonkey*, and I will be forever grateful for your time, dedication, and friendship. www.myindependenteditor.com ♥

Foreword

When I was a little girl, my mother decided to write a book about her life. For years, she jotted down her thoughts and feelings, in much the same way as one would in a journal or blog today. For fear of scorn from her family, she decided to put her dream aside.

I knew this troubled her deeply. In 2005, she decided to put her thoughts into words, and we began a series of interviews that lasted more than a year. We hoped this would keep her story intact so she could finish it one day. With that, *Weedmonkey* was born.

The process was hard on my mother. Many of the memories were painful, and she would break down as she relived them all over again. Old anger bubbled to the surface as she recalled the abuse she'd suffered. Mostly, though, it made her sad. Oftentimes we would have to stop, and it would be days before she felt able to continue.

In February 2006, my mother was diagnosed with terminal cancer and given three months to live. On her deathbed, she asked me to finish *Weedmonkey* for her.

She crossed over on April 30, 2006. She was 77.

With her heavenly guidance, I found her notes and our interviews, but it took me several years to put all the pieces together. Bits and pieces of the story were stashed in a collection of folders.

There were notes typed neatly on carbon paper, but most were handwritten, scribbled and scratched out memories, thoughts, and dreams. There were little torn pieces of paper with hastily jotted ideas on them. It was overwhelming.

It took a while, but out of love and dedication to the woman I called Ma, I fulfilled a deathbed promise.

These are her words but it was me who put them together.

I hope I have made her proud. ♥

I tried to look away. My mother was more beautiful in death than she had been in life.

I saw her body as I walked into the dimly lit room. I hated this moment, even though I'd known for two years she was dying.

We had made a promise to each other years ago that if either of us was diagnosed with a terminal illness, we would not keep it a secret from one another. My family was angry with me for telling her the truth when she asked me if she were dying, but I knew in my heart I had done the right thing.

I hesitated so my eyes could adjust to the semidarkness of the funeral home, and I stood in the hall longer than necessary to look at her in death. The slight hint of formaldehyde stung my nostrils. Someone had arranged the chairs in a semicircle, and people were gathering as I made my way inside to the room that held my mother's casket.

I stared at her. She had never looked more beautiful. She had always been the prettiest woman around, no matter where we lived. Her skin was translucent and as smooth as porcelain. Daddy used to call her his Dresden doll.

As I looked at her, I could not believe she was dead. I could not stop staring at the beautiful, lifeless body, certain that at any moment she would open her eyes and ask who all these people were and what they were doing there.

My brother's wife, Betty, had made all the necessary arrangements, and she'd chosen a soft blue suit and a white ruffled blouse that complimented my mother's auburn hair. I wondered if the back had been cut away. I'd read where they did that—dressed the dead in only the front half of the outfit—and it bothered me to think of my mother being buried in a backless suit.

I can't remember her even owning a full suit. A skirt, a jacket, but never a matching set.

My mother had always worn her thick, auburn hair down, cascading to her shoulders in deep, natural waves.

After the removal of her cancerous right lung and collarbone, she was unable to raise her arms to care for it in the manner in which she was accustomed, so it had been cut into a short, easy-to-care-for style. It had grown several inches since her last cut, making her look far younger than her fifty-eight years. Even the petite, frail hands crossed over her breast were pink and youthful looking.

I was startled when Betty walked over to my mother's casket, lifted the thin, white veil that covered her face, and placed her hand under the top opening of her blouse. "I wonder if they removed that tumor from her breast."

Then she pulled aside the blouse to reveal a purple, bell-shaped growth. I turned and walked away. How could she be so thoughtless? Didn't Betty know how I felt seeing that ugly cancerous tumor? For the rest of my life, every time I felt a pain in my chest I would wonder if it was the beginning of cancer.

I chose one of the end chairs facing the casket.

I tried to look away from the face that showed above the rim of the casket, but I couldn't stop staring at her.

The room was hot and the air heavy—a heaviness only death can bring. I wished someone would stop the clicking noises in the overworked air conditioner. That sound, when mixed with the soft organ music being piped in through Muzak, was almost vulgar.

Although I knew other people had come into the room, I was only now becoming aware of their presence. I looked around at the familiar faces. There wasn't a single person there who had not condemned my mother at one time or another. Now, however, they could only remember her virtues.

"Do you remember when Ester Rogers was in the hospital, and Maud took in her four children for over a month?"

"Remember when old man Jackson died, and there was no one to care for his wife? Maud went over every day and took her food and cared for her until her sister arrived from Ohio."

I looked around the room at them, each one of them, and I remembered their treatment of my mother. They had treated my mother—our family—like trash. Now, they were singing her praises.

There was Uncle Howard and Aunt Elizabeth, one of Daddy's sisters. Always so pious and right, Elizabeth had accused Uncle Howard of fathering my sister, Jewell. She told everyone in the family—and anyone else who would listen—that she had caught him and my mother together.

I don't know if the story was true or not; I was only five years old when Jewell was born.

There were Daddy's three other sisters. I remember when I was staying with my grandmother once and heard them call my mother a whore and discuss how terrible it was that their brother had married such a loose woman.

Funny . . . Each of them had born a child out of wedlock, and one of them had two. No one knew their fathers.

I wondered how much longer I could accept their tasteless pity.

As I sat there, trying to drown out the false sympathies that swirled around me, I suddenly remembered the time when I screamed at my mother, "I wish you would die!" I was young then, just fourteen, and death was so far away.

My grief strangled me like invisible hands clutching my throat. I had to leave. I could not look at her for another moment, could not gaze one single second longer at the pious faces around me. I had to get away before I did or said something I'd regret. But most of all, I couldn't face my own conscience.

Before I could flee, my Aunt Frances moved to the chair next to mine. Mom had once said of her, "Frances is a dangerous woman. A favor from her can do more harm than her scorn."

"Virgie, I cannot say that I'm sorry. In your mother's case, death was a blessing. She suffered so much and for so long. At last she is at peace."

I just looked at her, wishing she would go away. It made no difference to her that my mother was dead. She'd never cared for us. Not once were we invited to her home. Uncle Raymond was mayor and his sister, my mother, was married to a half-breed, a Cherokee. She couldn't risk offending his voters.

She continued. "Did you know that I cared for your mother when she was in the hospital?" I had forgotten Frances was a registered nurse. "It was sad what happened to her. Of course your father told you."

I turned to look at her. "I was only nine years old when Mom came home from the hospital, Aunt Frances. No one told me anything. I just remember they took my mother away and brought home a stranger."

"You mean they never told you anything about what happened to your mother?" she said in disbelief.

Apparently, she had forgotten that when I was growing up, a child of nine was usually told nothing except what adults felt they should know.

As a child growing up during the Depression, I learned not to ask questions. I got up, ate, went to school, came home, helped with the little ones, went to bed, and repeated the same routine the next day. Children were objects, *things*, and they never carried much weight in the world.

She shifted her heavy girth in the undersized chair. "It must have been terrible for you, living with her every day and not knowing." She sighed.

"I'll tell you as much as I know."

I braced myself for what I thought would be another bashing of my mother's memory.

"Do you remember anything about that time?" she asked, her wary gaze piercing me.

I *had* remembered. I remembered the day in the garden, the day I caught my mother having sex with a man who was not my father. That same man had fathered a child with her—my sister, Opal. *That* is what I remembered. I remembered my mother being in such a state after she saw me watching them, knowing, that she locked herself in the bedroom and wouldn't come out.

I remembered Daddy trying to break down the door, running around to the side of the house, and banging on the bedroom window yelling, "Maud, no!"

Then they took my mother away. When she came home, she was acting different, strange, and couldn't care for us like the mother we'd known before. My brother and I were placed in a foster home, and I never saw my baby sister again; she wasn't there when we returned. *That is what I remembered.*

But I just shook my head. I didn't dare tell her what I knew.

"Do you remember when your mother was taken to the hospital after her suicide attempt?"

"What? Her what? My mother never tried to kill herself! When?"

She hesitated and measured her words with care. "Oh Virgie, I can't believe no one told you."

I looked away from her. Was this just

another nail in my mother's coffin from this ungrateful family? *Was this the truth*?

She continued. "Do you want me to go on?"

I nodded.

"Virgie, did you know your mother had been pregnant again?"

I stared at her; I had not known.

"Well, whatever happened at the house that got her so upset caused her to hemorrhage. She miscarried while she was in the hospital. She was in such a fitful state that she was taken to the state mental hospital, where she was given . . . electric shock treatments."

I choked back tears of shock and disgust.

"While there, she became very ill, and her fever rose to 105. During the night, one of the nurses forgot to raise the bed rails. During a fit of fever, your mother fell out of bed and hit her head on the floor. She was unconscious for three days; on the fourth day, the doctors couldn't get a pulse or a heartbeat, and she was declared dead. They moved her to an empty room and notified her brother—you know, the one who is a minister. He was the closest relative near the hospital.

"After spending a half hour with your mother, he came running down the hall calling for a doctor. He said he was kneeling by her bed, praying, when he saw a movement under the sheet. He uncovered her face and saw a fluttering under her eyelids. I and the other two nurses ran to the room. We don't know what happened, but she had a pulse and a heartbeat. Ever so light, but it was there.

"We took her back to her room and waited.

Two days passed before she showed any signs of awareness. Your uncle had just left the room as I entered, and she asked me, 'Who was that man who was talking to me?'

"I was shocked to find that, not only did she not recognize her own brother, she did not recognize me. I thought her memory would return, but when your father came in and reached down to her, she screamed. He was a stranger to her, Virgie. After a battery of tests, we feared her memory loss might be permanent. I am so sorry…all these years and you didn't know."

I looked at her in disbelief. No, I had not known that the strange, seemingly uncaring woman my father had brought home from the hospital had little or no memory of him or their children.

Why hadn't someone told me?

I was nine years old at the time of my mother's illness. I would have understood enough to overlook rather than hate. If I had known, perhaps our lives would have been different.

Although I didn't care for my aunt, I was grateful to her for telling me what I should have been told long ago. All those years of hating my mother and wondering why she was so different, thinking she no longer loved us. Why hadn't someone told me?

I walked back over to my mother's casket. I looked at her and realized that I had been living with a stranger all those years. Sadly, I'd been a stranger to her, too.

Scenes flashed through my mind like colors in a kaleidoscope. Scenes without meaning, beginning, or ending. I'd spent my whole life hating my mother for an illness that I now knew was not her fault. My brother and sister were too young to remember her before her illness, but I remembered and the contrast was heartbreaking.

After the funeral, I returned to my brother's house. I wondered if I should tell him or if he already knew and had not told me. I decided to wait. My head ached with the knowledge of all the years I'd spent hating her, and now it was too late to start over.

I went into the bedroom. Betty had drawn the shades to protect her red velvet spread from the hot afternoon sun. I pulled down the bedspread and folded it over the foot of the bed. The cool cotton sheet was soothing to my weary, perspiring body. Praying for the throbbing in my head to stop, I drifted into a troubled and restless sleep.

I was grateful for the long drive back to Maryland. There were so many painful years of hate that I wanted to think about, relive, and try to understand. Years that had been locked away in the dusty attic of my memory—forever, I'd hoped—but now must be examined. I needed to light every corner, no matter how painful. I could not live the rest of my life without making peace with myself.

"Why, dear God, didn't someone tell me?" I cried out loud, but there was no one there to hear me.

The Beginning

I wondered what Daddy's feelings would be when he heard of Mom's death. She died knowing he never stopped loving her.

I missed Daddy. I had not seen him in eleven years, since he married Jenny and moved away from his family and friends. He had a new family of six children, and I always felt like an intruder when I went to see him. We'd been so close once. Now we were like strangers.

I could remember when we would talk for hours, but there seemed to be nothing left to say. Each time I saw him, he'd get tears in his eyes and ask about Mom.

Jesse Hopkins was born in 1908, the sixth child and third son born to Dicie, his Cherokee mother, and he was the most beautiful man I've ever seen. His eyes would laugh even when his face did not.

From his mother he inherited what she called "an understanding of the earth and its people," along with hair as black as night and beautiful dark skin that glistened in the sun. He claimed his smile had been given to him by the wind.

I loved to hear his stories. If I'd had a bad day or was in a foul mood, he would tell me one that always made me remember how precious life was. He'd say, "One day I was standing in the cornfield complaining that I had to work on such a beautiful day. I would have much rather been fishing than hoeing corn. Suddenly this big gust of wind came by. The wind looked down, saw the frown on my face, and said, 'My friend, why are you frowning? God gave you the gift of life. The world is beautiful, the sun is shining, the corn is tall, the birds are singing. Can you not hear them? They are singing for you. Are their songs falling on ears that do not hear? Is your heart not filled with love for your family and theirs for you? What else do you ask of life, my friend? What if God looks down on you and sees this young man who is unhappy with what he's been given? Perhaps God will fill his space with someone who would appreciate the gifts He has to give.'"

Daddy would always end his story by saying, "It is important to try to be happy with the things God has given us. There will be moments of sadness, but do not dwell on them; they will pass."

I don't know if I really believed all the stories he would tell me, but I never tired of listening to them. His grandmother had given him the Indian name Ki, and it seemed to fit him far better than the name given to him by his parents.

His mother, Dicie Woodwind, was a big-boned, full-blooded Cherokee with soft, brown eyes and a voice that would scare the hell out of you. When she spoke, you listened. She had a respectful, commanding presence. She had never cut her long, black hair—so long she could actually sit on it! She would roll it up into a big, round bun and pin it tightly to the back of her head. She had a wonderful sense of humor, and I loved her more than anyone else I knew, beside Daddy.

Born in 1883, she was one of eleven children. Her mother's family had been forced to leave their home in North Carolina and taken to a reservation in Oklahoma. She had often told me the story of The Trail of Tears.

This cruel act was a result of the enforcement of the Treaty of New Echota, an agreement signed under the provisions of the Indian Removal Act of 1830, in which the entire Cherokee Nation ceded its land east of the Mississippi River and agreed to move west to the Indian Territory.

Although neither the elected tribal leadership nor a majority of the Cherokee people ever accepted this act, the treaty was signed into law by President Andrew Jackson and was imposed by his successor, President Martin Van Buren, who allowed Georgian state troops to round up nearly 17,000 Cherokees in concentration camps before being sent to the West.

Most of the deaths occurred from diseases that spread within these camps before the relocation began.

She told of how, in 1838, the Cherokees were arrested, dragged at bayonet point from their homes in the cold October rain, and loaded like cattle into wagons that took them west. Many of them did not have blankets or moccasins.

Some slept in the wagons, others on the ground without a fire. Many mothers died of pneumonia, having given their own blankets to protect their children from the bitter cold. The hymn

"Amazing Grace" could often be heard floating gently on the wind as the displaced Indians tried to boost morale during the forced relocation, but it did not ease their suffering.

Most of the dead had to be left by the trailside, as the ground was too frozen to dig their graves. Their long, painful journey ended on March 26, 1839, almost six months and four thousand dead from North Carolina to Oklahoma.

My grandmother, born and raised on a reservation, told the story often so no one would forget what the white man had done to the American Indian.

She also told of the treatment of the Cherokee in the state of Georgia. Each month, unknown to the Cherokee family who lived there, a home would be offered as a raffle prize. Tickets were sold only to the white men. The holder of the winning ticket would move onto "his property," forcing the Cherokee family to leave.

The crimes that were committed against the American Indian would never be forgotten as long as my grandmother lived.

My grandfather, Peter, was a short, stocky, blue-eyed Dutchman who worked as a tool sharpener. Dicie was fifteen when they married, though it was never quite clear how the two of them met. They lived together many years, producing thirteen children. Their last, a daughter, was born prematurely and died three days after her birth.

I was always a little afraid of my grandmother. Her form of discipline was silence. If you disobeyed her, she would act as if you did not exist, you were "no longer in her range of vision." This form of punishment hurt worse than any switch on my backside.

She and my grandfather had gone into the hills of West Virginia where no human had ever set foot. They selected a section of land and began to homestead. Grandfather cut trees to form the logs for their home, and Mamaw made a mixture of mud, clay, and grass to mortar the logs.

One of her prized possessions was a string of rattlesnake rattles, called "buttons," which she had cut from the tails of the snakes that had bitten her while they were clearing the land. She kept the string of buttons hanging on the parlor wall to remind her of the "hard times."

I loved to hear my Aunt Mabel tell the story of the day her brother, my Uncle Chester, was born. One summer she had gone with my grandparents to clear rocks and weeds in their garden. After they'd been working for about hour, Mamaw called to Aunt Mabel to follow her.

My grandmother stopped at a towering oak tree several feet from where Grandfather was working. She removed her apron and spread it on the ground. Then she lifted the many skirts she wore and sat on the apron. Aunt Mabel thought it strange for her mother to stop before her work was finished. With her eyes closed, Mamaw sat with her back and head resting against the trunk of the tree.

Aunt Mabel thought she'd fallen asleep, but her mother sat up suddenly, lifted her skirt, tore off a section of her white petticoat, and began to clean a red, wrinkled, black-haired baby boy. She had not uttered a sound.

My grandmother removed a knife from the pocket of her skirt and swiftly cut the umbilical cord. She ripped off the remaining portion of her petticoat, wrapping it tightly around her newborn son, and instructed Aunt Mabel to take him to the cabin and to stay with him until she returned.

As Aunt Mabel walked up the hill to the cabin, she looked back to see her mother returning to the field to finish her day's work. Her father had not once looked up from his work and was apparently unaware of his son's birth.

* * *

My mother, Maud Ward, and had been raised in a background so different from my father's that I couldn't understand how they'd ever gotten together.

Maud was born in 1910 into a wealthy, genteel, southern family on the Tarragon plantation, located on 3,600 acres of prime North Carolina land. She was raised by a black nanny she affectionately called Mama Louise. Her father, Robey Ward—or Rich, as the townspeople referred to him—employed a number of black men and women whose fathers had been slaves at Tarragon when he was a child. They were devoted to him, and Tarragon was the only home they'd ever known. These workers were never regarded as slaves or disrespected in any way. Robey referred to them as "his people" and they respected him. In fact, they each had their own home on the plantation. Her father also owned the only hotel and emporium in Valley of The Crosses, North Carolina.

Maud's mother, Mallie, was a petite, frail woman who spoke in a soft, whispering voice and was a devoted wife and mother. Her only regret was that she had wanted to become an actress, but it was unthinkable in those days for a nice girl to have aspirations for the stage. Two weeks after graduating from Mrs. Wilson's School for Girls, she and Robey Ward were married at Tarragon.

Until the age of eleven, my mother lived in an atmosphere of charm and wealth, but the death of her mother changed all that.

At the age of thirty-three and after the birth of her seventh child, Mallie died of complications of childbirth. Robey blamed himself for her death.

Their doctor had cautioned him many times that he should protect her from having more children. After her death, he turned to alcohol to numb his guilt. In his drunken stupor, he told anyone who would listen how he'd killed his beloved Mallie because he had loved her too much.

After months of neglect and unpaid bills, Tarragon was sold at auction. Each child was placed with a relative. Everyone said, "It's just until Robey gets back on his feet. He's still mourning for Mallie. He'll soon be back on top again; you can't keep a good man like Robey Ward down." But he never stopped mourning the loss of his Mallie.

A few months later, the emporium and hotel

were closed and the contents sold. The proceeds from the sale were divided among the relatives caring for Robey and Mallie's children.

As I got older, my grandfather would talk to me about Mallie, and the melody of tears would fill his eyes. I would sit quietly, knowing that while I didn't always understand everything he was telling me, I was sharing a precious part of his private world.

After our talks, he would get up, brush off his overalls, grasp my hand, smile down at me and say, "You are so much like my Mallie. When you smile, I see her in your face. When you laugh, I hear her voice. It's true that we live forever through our grandchildren."

As time passed, I didn't visit him as often. At the time of his death, I hadn't seen him in many years. I was saddened to hear of his passing, but I was also glad. Now, once again, he would be with his beloved Mallie.

Maud was placed with an uncle who owned a boardinghouse, where she worked in the kitchen and dining room each morning and after school to earn her keep.

One spring afternoon, my father stopped at the boardinghouse to spend the night. He was visiting his mother who had returned to her birthplace in North Carolina.

Daddy often told me the story of how he met "the most beautiful girl I had ever seen. I fell in love with your mother the first time I saw her. I thought she was the prettiest girl then, and I still think so. She had the most beautiful red hair, and she looked so tiny and afraid. When I first spoke to her, she pretended not to hear me, but I caught her looking at me. You should have seen her blush when I winked at her."

At that point in the story, my mother would always stop him. "Oh hush, Jesse, what will the children think?"

Daddy would slap her on the backside and reply, "They'll think that their father loves their mother. That is what they'll think. So stop your fussin', woman, and get me some dinner." Mom always pretended that she didn't like his teasing, but the look that passed between them told their true love story.

On a beautiful June day in 1928, seventeen-year-old Maud married nineteen-year-old Jesse. Mom had pleaded with her father to stand with her and to share her joy. But his only reply was, "I am not going to acknowledge any daughter of mine who marries a half-breed." She had hoped that he might change his mind, and she was saddened to see that not one of her family members was present at her wedding.

Prior to their marriage, Daddy had sustained himself by working any job available to him. Now married with a wife, he wanted a job with more responsibility and more income. He hoped to build a suitable home for Maud so she would not be shamed before her family. As long as he didn't aspire to more than the most menial of jobs, he didn't encounter any difficulty from the prejudiced public.

Daddy knew that most people in Valley of the Crosses did not like the Indians or the coloreds, but he had always minded his own business, did the job he was paid to do, and bothered no one. Once, he saw a cardboard sign in the window of the general store advertising for a clerk, so he decided to apply for the position.

As he started up the steps, the owner, seated on a wooden bench beside the door so he could hawk his wares to passersby, spit a stream of brown liquid across the porch railing and extended his left foot to cover the entrance to the store. “Hey, boy, if you got any notions of asking for that there job, forget it. I don't hire any niggers here.”

Living in the remote hills of West Virginia, Daddy had never suffered the hurt and humiliation of prejudice. He had never been subjected to the outside world and its cruelties. His neighbors and friends had also been of Indian heritage, and it was not the way of his people to hate anyone.

Upon facing the storeowner, Daddy straightened his shoulders, lifted his chin, and with pride looked directly into the man's eyes. “I am not a colored man. I am Cherokee, and if you were to offer me your job, I would not accept it. I would not work for a man such as you. My pride would not allow me to.”

The man laughed and spit another stream of tobacco across the front of my father's shoes. “Cherokee? That’s a laugh. Half the niggers in North Carolina claim to be Cherokee. Anyway, I would rather hire a nigger than a greasy-smelling Indian.”

As Daddy turned to leave, the man called after him. “If you really want to work, go up to Old Chloe Creek Hollow and ask for Joe Hicks. He's looking for someone to help him on his place, and I understand he's not too particular who it is as long as he works.” As Daddy walked away, he could hear the old man laughing between spits. “Cherokee my ass. He’s a nigger if I ever saw one.”

As the weeks passed, Daddy was still cleaning out stables, outhouses, and barnyards, painting fences, digging graves, burying the dead, and doing any work that had been delegated by the townspeople to be done by the coloreds and the Indians.

Jobs that were too good for the white men.

Majestic, Kentucky

In their third year of marriage, Mom became pregnant with me.

Once again burying his pride, Daddy tried to find a better job. One day, after his fourth rejection, he started across the street to avoid the old man from the general store. As he stepped onto the roadway, the man called out to him. “Hey, boy, you still looking for a job? I still don't like niggers or injuns, but I hear you’re a helluva good worker. That job is still open down at the store if you want it.” Daddy walked closer to him.

“I can't pay you much. A dollar a day is about all I can do. But I have a spare room in the back of the store where you and your squaw can stay.” He extended his hand. “My name is Hall, Seth Hall. Mr. Hall to you. What name do you go by?”

Mr. Hall dropped his hand when it became apparent that Daddy wasn't going to shake his. His people only extended their hand to a friend.

He lifted his head and replied, “My name is Hopkins, Jessie Ki Hopkins. Mr. Hopkins to you. Before I take your job there’s something I’d like to get straight with you. My wife is not a squaw. She was born at Tarragon. Her father is Robey Ward.”

Seth Hall looked at him in disbelief. “You tryin' to tell me you’re the Indian that married old Rich Ward's daughter? My God, I've known Rich Ward for nigh on to thirty years, and I never saw him so mad as when he told me his daughter had married some nig . . ."

For some reason, he decided to spare my daddy the dirty details. "Well, there's no use going into all the things he said, but he was sure mad as all get-out. Is it true that he disowned her? Of course it doesn't make a tinker's damn now. Since Mallie passed away, he's lost everything he ever owned. I don't think he has anything left to leave anyone anyway. Well, you want to work for me or not?"

Daddy nodded, and from that day on, they referred to each other as Mr. Hall and Mr. Hopkins.

The months that Jesse worked for Seth Hall were happy ones for Mom. She bought red calico from the store and made curtains for their room and a matching spread for the table. Daddy had whitewashed the walls and filled in the cracks with clay. He had made many friends in Valley of the Crosses. The townspeople no longer referred to him as "that injun."

He had built a reputation for being an honest, hardworking man, one who would never ask or beg for anything. It was the way of his people. Too many months of living in the white man's world had taught him to remain silent.

Mom was in her eighth month of pregnancy when she awoke to hear the news that Seth had died in his sleep. He'd never told them that he'd known for months that he would never see another summer. They would miss him, despite their differences; he had been a good friend.

Mom and Daddy managed the store until a cousin of Mr. Hall's arrived from Kentucky to claim his inheritance. A few days after his arrival, he placed a For Sale sign in the store window. It never occurred to Daddy that the new owner might sell. Mom and Daddy had hoped that the new owner might let them manage the store for him. Mr. Hall's cousin informed Daddy that he would return to Kentucky in ten days, and if the store had not been sold by then, he would have to close down the business and turn it over to an agent.

When the ten days had passed and the store was not sold, Daddy hired a man with a horse and wagon to take them to Chloe Creek with hopes of finding employment with Mr. Hicks.

The anguish of being without a job and his concern for Mom and their unborn child pained Daddy deeply. They had no choice but to make the long trip up to Chloe Creek. He made a pallet of quilts on the bed of the wagon to cover the rough unfinished boards. He removed his jacket, folded it, and placed it under Mom's head for a pillow.

With each lurch of the wagon, Mom would grasp her stomach, holding her baby closer to her body to protect it from harm.

As they traveled the dusty, unpaved road, Daddy reminisced about the plans he'd made for the three of them. He had wanted so much for Mom and their baby. He had planned a plankboard house with at least two bedrooms, maybe three. He had even drawn the plans for it on the back of a brown paper sack. He had never shown them to Mom; he'd wanted it to be a surprise for their first anniversary.

But now, headed into their third year, he didn't even have a job. He had planned to buy Mom some new dresses for after the baby came. He knew she had traded some of the fine dresses and hats she'd brought with her from Tarragon so they could have dishes and linens. As he thought of this tender, selfless gesture, he reached over for her hand. She opened her eyes and smiled as though she knew his thoughts. She placed her hand in his as they rode along. His heart raced at the tenderness of her touch.

He wished words were easier for him; there was so much he wanted to say to her. He hoped that she understood his quiet way and that she knew how much he loved her. Often at night he felt the moisture on her cheeks and knew that she had been crying. He, too, felt her pain and prayed, "Dear God, please don't ever let her stop loving me. I would not want to live without her beside me."

Daddy looked up as the driver called back to him. "Well, this is it. You go up the road apiece, and you'll see an old house on the side of the hill. It's the only one there; you can't miss it. I can't take my horses any closer. Old Man Hicks keeps a bunch of dogs up there, and they spook my horses every time I go anywhere near that place."

As he drove away, he called over his shoulder, "You better watch them dogs. They've been trained to kill niggers." Daddy opened his mouth to reply, but changed his mind. He'd learned long ago that it wouldn't make any difference.

Although he'd made some friends in town, most of the locals still considered the Indians and the coloreds to be one and the same. He certainly couldn't count on the dogs to tell the difference.

Daddy looked at the narrow walkway that was more of a path than a road. He looked at the boxes that contained all their worldly possessions, their life. As few as they were, he knew they couldn't carry all of them up to the Hicks' farm. He separated the boxes until he found one that contained their nightclothes and a change of clothing for the next day. He hid the remaining boxes behind the bushes, to be retrieved in the morning.

Mom tired easily, and they had to stop every few feet to allow her to rest. As darkness fell, it was impossible to see. Daddy's nostrils flared as he picked up the lingering scent of fried country ham. His stomach growled at the prospect of being fed. Mom had not once complained, but he knew she was also hungry. They hadn't eaten since early that morning.

He held her hand and tried to support her body, swollen and bulky with child, as they stumbled through the high weeds and thick clumps of crabgrass that grew where the road had once been. As the darkness closed in around them like a black cloud, Daddy moved closer to Mom, putting his arm around her waist. Though the evening air was cool, her back was wet with perspiration.

Suddenly they heard the barking of dogs. Their eyes searched the darkness in the direction of the sounds. They could make out the outline of a house, almost hidden by a dense cluster of trees. Out of the shadows came a light and a voice. "Who's out there? Make yourself known or I'll shoot!"

"I'm Jesse Hopkins with my wife. I need a job, and someone in Valley of the Crosses told me you were looking for help."

The old man came closer and shoved the lantern first in Daddy's face and then Mom's. "Well, you look all right. Come on up to the house. Have you had any vittles? I don't have a woman around. She up and died on me nigh onto two years ago. Never gave me any young'uns, but she was a good worker. She could outwork any man I ever had on this place. Good cook, too. I cook all right, nothin' fancy, but I sure miss her cookin'."

After a meal of corn bread and leftover ham fat washed down with buttermilk, the old man picked up his lantern. "I guess you folks want to turn in. You look mighty tired, little lady. Didn't notice at first that you were expecting. Looks like that young'un is ready to show his face any day now. I got a little house across the road where you two can stay. We'll talk in the morning."

He led them to a one-room log cabin in a field of weeds that almost covered the windows. In the dim light of the lantern Mr. Hicks had given them, they found an old iron bed and a stack of blankets folded on a chair. Exhausted, they fell asleep to the sound of crickets and frogs and what seemed to be a million other nighttime voices.

Daddy was awakened by the sound of Mom's urgent whispers. "Jess, there's something in our bed. Get the light." Daddy reached for the lantern that he'd placed by his bedside. As he lifted it, he heard the sound of something falling to the floor. He reached for his matches to light the lantern, and as his eyes adjusted to the dimly lit room, he stared in disbelief. The room was alive with snakes—crawling up the walls, between the logs, and on and under the bed. A trio of them slithered atop the mirror of an old dresser. He could feel the bed vibrating from the uncontrollable quivering of Mom's tender body.

Her low sobbing grew into hysterical screams that filled the night air. The once carefree crickets were silenced.

Using the stub of an old broom he found in the corner, Daddy hit, chased, and beat at the snakes until he'd cleared the cabin. He rushed to Mom's side of the bed to find her writhing in pain. "Jessie, the baby is coming! Please get me out of this place. I don't want our baby to be born in a place like this. Please, Jesse, hurry!"

He picked up her trembling body to find her water had broken and her gown was wet. He wrapped the blanket around her and walked across the road to Mr. Hicks' place. He let them in and gave them a bed to sleep in.

At the first ray of early morning light, Daddy tiptoed out of the room, leaving the door ajar so he could hear if Mom called to him. He followed the sounds coming from the kitchen. "Well, good morning there, young fellow," Mr. Hicks said as Daddy entered the room. "You and your little lady really had a bad night, didn't you? How's she doin'?"

Daddy reached for the cup of coffee Mr. Hicks had placed on the table in front of him.

“She's asleep now. She stopped crying about an hour ago. That cabin of yours almost scared her to death. Did you know it was full of snakes? Unless you have something better than that for us to live in, I'm afraid we can’t stay. I can’t expect my wife and baby to live in a place like that.”

The old man laughed. “Yeah, I knew there were some, but they’re just plain ol’ black snakes, boy. Wouldn’t hurt a soul. Most of ’em have been living here longer than I have. Now don't you go worrying about them snakes. I'll go over with you later, and we'll fix up the cabin so they don't get in. Right now you gotta worry about that little lady in there. I'll tell you what we'll do. You finish up your breakfast and get some for your woman if she wants it. I have to go into town, and I’ll stop by the Henderson place and send Martha back to birth your baby. She births all the babies around these parts. Don't fret none; she'll be here before dinner time.”

Daddy spent the next two hours sitting with Mom, who drifted in and out of a restless, pain-filled sleep. When Mrs. Henderson arrived, he was glad to relinquish his bedside chair to her. He hadn’t heard her come into the room and commented on her stealthy entrance.

She threw back her head and roared with a laughter that shook the pictures on the wall. “I scared you, did I? Well, my pappy was an Indian; Cherokee he was. Well, I'm here to tell you that no one could sneak up on a rabbit like he could. He would have that critter half skinned before it even knew it was dead.”

Once again her hearty laugh echoed through

the tiny farmhouse.

"Mr. Hicks tells me your wife is about ready for birthin'. You go out and do whatever you have to do. There's no place for a man in here; you'll just get in the way." Daddy stooped down and kissed Mom's wet forehead. She looked so tiny and pale. He vowed that he would never put her through so much pain again.

After thirty-six hours of hard labor, the midwife told Daddy to go into town to get the doctor. The larger town of Majestic, Kentucky, was four miles away, and Daddy walked the rough and rocky road into town. The doctor was available and soon headed out on horseback.

Since his horse could only accommodate one person, Daddy had to walk back to the farmhouse where Mom and the midwife were waiting.

I was born dead on March 17, 1929, wrapped in a blanket, and laid on the table far from Mom's sight. As the doctor and midwife left, they met Mamaw on the road. She'd come into town looking for Mom and Daddy and was told that he'd come to the farm looking for work.

My grandmother did not trust the white man or his ways. She had traveled the long distance from Valley of the Crosses to be of aid to my mother. Her keen sense of knowing brought her there at the precise time Mom was in need.

When the doctor told Dicie that her granddaughter was stillborn, she didn't believe him and scoffed, "Damn stupid white doctors! They know nothin' about birthin' an Indian baby."

She arrived at the farmhouse to find my lifeless little body on the table, wrapped in the birthing sheet. Mom was alone and grieving. Mamaw unwrapped the bloody sheet and removed the thin veil of skin that covered my face. She prepared two pans of water—one hot and one cold.

She dipped me first in one and then the other, back and forth, smacking me on the behind all the while. Mom said I was black and blue by the time I began to breathe and wail.

After I was born, Daddy and Mr. Hicks took a good look at the cabin in the broad daylight. It was in worse shape than Daddy had imagined.

There was no way in the world he could allow Mom and me to live in such a place. He needed the work, but we also needed a decent place to live. He could see now why Mr. Hicks had trouble finding someone to work there. Mr. Hicks was kind enough to allow Mom into his house to give birth, but allowing us to live with him was another story.

Daddy decided his only option was to take us back into town to find more work and a suitable place to live. He took their one packed box and Mom carried me as they made their way back down the road they'd traveled the night before.

At the last minute, Daddy decided to go into the town of Hopewell, West Virginia. He had heard there might be work there and decided to take the chance.

They had walked for about two miles when a truck stopped and offered them a ride into

Hopewell. The driver let them off at the courthouse.

There was a large gathering of men around a sign that had been posted on the courthouse door. Daddy made his way to the front of the crowd.

The sign read: *Good, strong, hardworking men wanted to work in new coal mine in West Virginia. Transportation furnished, housing available. Train leaving at 3:00 today.*

Stotesbury, West Virginia

My brother, Wade, was born in Stotesbury, West Virginia, in 1931, when I was two years old. We used to call him Jug since he was as stubborn as an old mule and had a head as hard as a moonshine jug.

Named for prominent investment banker Edward T. Stotesbury, the coal mining town flourished during the 1930s.

We shared an apartment house with four other families. Our two-room apartment was on the ground floor and had a tiny porch where Mom would shake out the rugs and hang them along the railing to air out.

Our building was alive with music most of the time, as Mom and Daddy would gather on the front porch with the other tenants and play the Jew's harp and sing.

Once a week, a man known as the Jewel Tea man would come to deliver cakes and bread. We would save up our coupons and redeem them for prizes.

The Jewel Company, a door-to-door delivery service for coffee, was founded in Chicago in 1899, and in 1902, became known as the Jewel Tea Company. In 1934, Jewel Food merged with Jewel Tea and became more of a grocery delivery service. We always looked forward to the Jewel Tea man's visits.

Daddy worked in the coal mines while Mom took care of the house and her two active children.

Every morning, the company truck would pick up Daddy and the other men who worked in the mines. Although Mom was glad that Daddy had a good job, she was scared to death of him working underground in the mines.

Every time the siren would blow, we would all run down to the mine opening to see which miner would be carried out or walk out on his own.

Mom said there were cave-ins, poisonous gases, and explosions to worry about. Although we were young, she never hesitated to show her fears or concerns to us children. In turn, that made us even more afraid.

When I got older, I asked Daddy about it, and he explained that the most dangerous thing in the mine was methane gas. It was explosive, and you couldn't smell it or taste it. It's lighter than air, so it rose to the top of the mines. Daddy said if they could find out where it was, they piped in fresh air to dilute the gas. It made me feel a little better to hear that.

But I didn't like it when he told me they used canaries to test for gases in the mines. He said they were very sensitive to the gas, and if they detected it, they would chirp and sing and make noise all day. But if the gas levels got too high, the canaries would be unable to breathe and they would die. If they stopped singing, the miners knew that the gas levels were too high and would leave the mines quickly so they would not be caught in an explosion.

Daddy also told me about the workers known as firemen who were paid to disperse the gas in the mines by setting it on fire. These brave men would walk down the dark mine tunnels carrying a long stick with a candle on the end and ignite any gas they encountered. An explosion would occur, and if not dressed properly, the worker could be killed.

Another danger of the mines was poor ventilation. As the mines got deeper, oxygen was in short supply and the miner's would die if they couldn't get enough air to breathe.

As we got older, the constant worry about strikes, layoffs, mine closings, and working for companies that placed more emphasis on profits than on safety became everyday concerns for us.

Daddy would come home every night covered in coal dust. Oftentimes, I couldn't tell one man from the other, all black and dusty. It wasn't until after they'd showered that I recognized my father. I was his little shadow and followed him everywhere. I would sit on the stairs while he showered, and he would talk to me through the curtain. I hung on every word as he talked about his day in the mines.

Daddy made friends with one of the men, Ethan Allan, who gave us a pet German shepherd named Jack. If one of us needed something from the store, we would put a note on Jack's collar and he'd walked to the store. The clerk would put the item in a bag and attach it to Jack. All the neighbors wanted to buy the dog from us, but Daddy said no.

One day, Daddy couldn't find Jack. We looked for days, but he never came home. After a week, Daddy found him down by the creek. He'd been poisoned and left to die. We sure missed old Jack; he was a good friend.

* * *

I remember Mom talking about the two churches in town—one for the whites and one for the coloreds. We would go to church every Sunday without fail. When Daddy was baptized, I cried because I thought he was being drowned by the preacher.

Daddy and Ethan had a vegetable garden on the left-hand side of the road, across from the railroad tracks. They were very proud of that garden and worked on it every chance they got. One rainy day, he and Ethan went to pull weeds since the ground would be soft. Ethan was standing several feet above Daddy; I was watching them from the truck.

Suddenly, a line of high-tension wires broke loose from an overhead pole and went flying across the garden. One broke and came down and grabbed Ethan around the waist and pulled him high into the air. He was dragged across the field. After the initial screams, the only sound was the crackling and sparks that came from the wire around Ethan's body as it swung him back and forth in midair like a rag doll.

He was too far for Daddy to reach him, and when he came back down to the ground, he was burnt and dead. Daddy got back into the truck, and we drove into town for help.

After the funeral, Daddy was so sad that he never went back up to the garden, and he never replanted in the spring. He was a long time getting over Ethan's death.

* * *

My first memory of Mom was an ugly one and began a lifelong resentment toward her that grew deeper as I got older.

Upstairs in the apartment building was a little girl named Rosebud. She was just a tiny thing, still in a highchair. Their apartment had a balcony that hung over our porch and she would always throw her toys over the side. I would pick up the toys and take them back to her.

One day when I came in with her toys in my hand, she began screaming at the top of her lungs. Her mother thought I had taken them from her, when in fact I was returning them after their flight over the balcony. She reported this falsehood to Mom, who acted quickly in her punishment. I had never seen her so angry. I was spanked repeatedly until blood oozed from my legs.

I was dragged downstairs to our apartment and told to wait for Daddy to come home.

When he arrived, he questioned her about the cuts on my legs. My resentment toward her began right then and there. I was four years old. Daddy took me in the other room and put salve on my legs to soothe them.

Later, Mom told me she felt bad for whipping me like that when I kept telling her I was innocent. She said she was sorry she didn’t believe me.

I wish she had taken me in her arms when it happened and told me that. I remember feeling resentment and a desire for revenge. It is horrifying now, as an adult, to think a child of that age could harbor such feelings.

My chance for revenge came one day when the bakery deliveryman was making his usual stops at the apartment house. For some reason, he seemed to make more stops at ours. I didn't like him.

Once I saw him pinch Mom on the backside, and another time he put his hand on her breast. It made me angry. She giggled like a schoolgirl, different from the way she would act with Daddy, and he would always give us cakes, although we couldn't afford them.

Once, she saw me watching them, and she backed away, her eyes on mine. They moved to the other side of the kitchen, talking in low tones so I couldn’t hear what was being said. But I didn’t care; the fact that he had touched Mom in any way was enough to anger Daddy.

One day while he was there, he gave me a cookie, and Mom sent me outside to play. We had three steps down to the landing on our porch, and the yard was shaped like a triangle. At the end of the yard was an area for trash cans.

I was standing there, looking at the trash, trying to understand why Mom had sent me outside. I had never been sent out there when the bakery man came before, but this time she practically pushed me out the door.

Although I was wearing a wool coat, I was freezing, and I'd had no breakfast other than the cookie. I wanted to go back inside to get warm, but Mom had locked the door. I tried several times to get back in, but there was no answer as I knocked, so I went back into the yard.

One of the women nearby came out to set out a trash barrel for pickup. "Virgie, what are you doing outside this early in the morning? Where are your hat and gloves, and where is your mother?" She looked at the bread truck parked in front of the building.

"Would you like to come inside and have some hot chocolate?" I wanted to go with her. I was cold, and I liked hot chocolate, but I knew if Mom came out and found me gone, she would be very angry. I just shook my head and thanked her.

After she went back inside, I walked over to the trash can. Someone had thrown a box of matches on top of the cans. I opened it and found that it still contained several wooden matchsticks. I knew how to strike them, as I had seen Daddy light his pipe many times. I took some paper from one of the cans and placed it on the ground. The first match did not ignite. The second one flared up, catching the paper in a bright yellow-red flame.

As the fire died down, I would add more and more paper from the trash can. Soon I wasn't cold anymore. As I stood there warming my hands, I was startled to hear someone scream at me from an upstairs window. The tail of my coat had touched the little paper fire, and the wool coat went up in flames with me in it. I screamed as the fire neared my hair and face. Several of the mothers ran to me and wrapped me in a rug my mother had left hanging on the porch rail. They rolled me on the ground to put out the flames.

I heard one of them ask, “Where on earth is her mother?”

One woman replied, “Where do you think she is? Look who's parked out front.”

Mom came running from the house, undressed except for her gown. She hugged me to her, trying to soothe my crying, but I ran from her. “It's your fault! It’s your fault, and I'm going to tell Daddy when he comes home!”

The other women stood in a group, whispering at the obvious, as the bakery man made his exit, whistling as he got into his truck and drove away.

I was very angry with Mom and couldn't wait until Daddy came home so I could tell him. I was a devious child, and I told her, “You just wait till I tell Daddy on you!”

After Daddy's shower, we came back up the stairs hand in hand. Mom looked at me, wondering if I had told him anything. We all gathered at the dinner table, and Daddy's eyes widened at the beautiful chocolate cake Mom brought in for dessert.

“Maud, I wish you wouldn’t buy these cakes. You know we can't afford this sort of thing. Besides, I like the ones you bake much better.” I knew Mom didn't have to pay for that cake—not with money, anyway.

"They made me go outside!" I blurted out.

Then I told him how my coat had caught on fire, and how the women rolled me in the rug, and how Mom had come out of the house in her nightgown and the bakery man drove away in his truck. I told him everything and then looked at Mom for a reaction.

My feelings of triumph turned to fear when I looked at Daddy. He didn't say a word; he didn't have to. His eyes said it all. The Cherokee way was silence. He rose from the table, pushed in his chair, and walked out the back door. I could see him light his pipe as he sat down on the steps.

I looked at Mom, fearful of punishment from her. She just stared at me for a long time with tears falling down her cheeks.

After that, Daddy asked the mines for a transfer, and we relocated to Marytown, West Virginia. There, we lived in a four-room house owned by the mining company. It was better than living in the apartment; however, we had an outside toilet which took us a little while to get used to, especially for Mom who had grown up in luxury at Tarragon.

She had only been in an outhouse once, several years before. She had been visiting a friend from school who had married and moved into the country.

It had been a long journey that day, and Mom had to use the bathroom. Taking me with her, she sat me down next to her on some newspapers that were lying next to the opening she was using. To her horror, she turned to see that I had fallen into the dark hole and was now half submerged in the muck below. She reached down toward my outstretched hands but could not reach me as I sank lower and lower into the human waste. She ran from the outhouse screaming. Several of the men had to push the shed over in order to rescue me.

I loved Mom, but I found myself doing things to cause trouble for her. She was a cleaning freak, and no matter where we lived, the house always smelled like lye. She would get a big metal tub and mix the solution with hot water and would bleach the floors until they gleamed.

Once she left the metal tub in the bedroom where I was playing. A favorite game of mine was spinning. I would spin and spin around until I was so dizzy I would fall over. While she was in the kitchen, I was in the bedroom spinning and fell over into the tub of hot lye water. I screamed, and when Mom came running, she screamed right along with me.

Hearing the commotion, the neighbors rushed over and wrapped me in a wet sheet. They used tweezers to pull the burnt skin off my fragile little body. Mom ran to the mines and got Daddy, who scolded her for not paying attention to me and allowing me to get hurt.

I have many other memories of my mom from those days in West Virginia. Mom used to listen to the soap operas on the radio and she absolutely loved *Young Dr. Malone* and *Helen Trent*. All the shows were sponsored by soap companies, and my very first word was "Rinso."

Mom had a breathtaking beauty that could rival any movie star, and I always admired the way she took care of herself. She had a trim figure and enjoyed showing everyone how she could still wear the belt of my younger brother. She took regular naps during the day or would just lie down for an hour or so, and we were taught to respect this time she set aside for herself. We would never think of bothering her unless it was an emergency.

In comparison, the other women in the area always looked tired and irritable and had let themselves grow fat. They often looked as if they didn't bathe often. It was no surprise that they were jealous of Mom and kept a close eye on their husbands when she was around.

Mom was a nervous woman who occupied her time by being afraid. She talked often of her fear of Bonnie and Clyde, although according to the radio, they were several states away. When they were killed in Louisiana in 1934, she was visibly relieved.

I loved my mother, and although we had our differences, she was a kind and loving woman. She had a gentle demeanor and tried to do the best she could during the hard times of the Great Depression.

Mom was not used to the type of life Daddy provided for us. I often wondered at times if she didn't regret marrying him and disobeying her father. She could have had the luxury of living at Tarragon and being a wealthy man's wife who had servants to wait on her and clean her home. But instead, she fell in love with a dirt-poor Cherokee, and she spent her days bleaching wooden floors.

Each time I asked her how much she loved me, she always answered the same way: “a bushel and a peck and a hug around the neck.”

Coalwood, West Virginia

Coalwood, West Virginia, was the product of George LaFayette Carter, one of the few natives of Appalachia to strike it rich shortly after the Civil War when industrialization came to the mountains.

The eldest of nine children of a disabled Confederate veteran, Carter married his storekeeper boss's daughter and went on to become a shrewd and wealthy businessman.

In 1905, he bought20,000 acres in McDowell County, West Virginia, and out of the wilderness, began building the industrial community he named Coalwood.

By the 1930s, the town was nationally recognized as a model town, and the houses were painted and surrounded by flower gardens and nice lawns. There was a wide variety of people living in Coalwood: Bohemians, Croatians, Syrians, Slavs, Germans, and Americans. It was quite different from the last mining town we'd lived in. Daddy worked at Consolidation Coal Company and said the town was a reflection of who owned the mines.

By the time we moved to Coalwood, I was five and Jug was three. My sister, Jewell, had been born in 1934, and was a year old when we made the move. As a twelve-pound baby, she'd kicked a hole in Mom's uterus, and Mom was given ether for the intense pain.

In Coalwood, we lived in a three-room, L-shaped house. We had a kitchen and two bedrooms.

The house was built right into the side of the mountain, and dirt had been dug out for the yard.

When we first moved in, we had a large front yard. But one spring, we were sitting on the porch where we would all gather during warm weather. Unknown to us, the mountain snow and ice would melt each spring and become first a trickling creek and then a swiftly flowing river. The front yard washed away, and we even had water under the front porch.

A German family named Klaus lived next door to us and had a son named Buster who was a mining inspector. He was tall and quite dashing in his Outback hat and boots that stretched up his long, lean legs to his knees.

Every day, I would walk home from school for lunch, and I loved that Mom would always have it ready for me when I arrived. On this particular day, when Mom reached into the kitchen cabinet for bread, she let out a bloodcurdling scream. Inside the cabinet was a long black snake.

Buster had also come home for lunch, and he ran inside our house when he heard Mom scream.

I stood on a chair and watched the snake swirl around on the bleached-out kitchen floor. To my amazement, Buster grabbed the snake and put it outside. That little act of heroism turned into an affair with Mom. I knew about it, and I was forced to keep her secret.

Daddy would leave early in the morning while the sky was still dark. He was a slate picker, which was hard and nasty work. All day long, the men had to bend over a conveyor belt and pick out the slate and coal that had too much rock in it before the good coal was sorted into different sizes for shipment to the steel mills.

He wouldn't return until way after dark when we kids were already in bed. Jug and I shared a bedroom, while baby Jewell slept in the room with Mom and Daddy.

Our windows were close to the ground, and one night I saw Buster outside with his lips pressed up against the window. Mom was inside with her lips in the same position on the inside of the glass. I didn't know if this was a regular thing or not, but I didn't like it, and I couldn't understand how she could hurt Daddy this way over and over again.

Mom had been unable to find common ground to form friendships with the other wives in the coal mining camps where we lived. Alone, beautiful, and in need of companionship, she turned to other men to satisfy her needs.

In the beginning, these were harmless flirtations. Daddy pretended not to notice. He was secretly proud that the other men found his wife attractive, and he was happy to hear her laughter. He knew he had not made her happy and that he had disappointed her in many ways. He had hoped his love for her would be enough.

When he found out that her flirting had led to an affair with Buster, he took his knife into the woods, determined to end his pain. But, filled with love for her and his children, he could not let go. Not yet.

Her affairs continued, and though he knew everyone thought him a fool, he couldn't bring himself to leave her for good. He managed to leave several times over the years, but he couldn't stay away for long. Each time he returned, he tried harder to understand why he couldn't make her happy.

When her affair with Buster led to her becoming pregnant with baby Opal, he said nothing, but his pain was far greater than my mother's was at the birth of her daughter in 1936.

As if that wasn't enough to make me hate my mother, she showed me a cruel side unlike anything I'd seen before.

We had a dog named Eddie who we thought was a boy until *he* had a litter of eight puppies. She died giving birth to the last one; the poor thing died with a puppy still inside her.

I was too young to understand that newborn puppies couldn't live without their mothers. I wanted to keep them and take care of them, but they needed their mother's milk and attention.

The morning after Eddie died I went to school but looked forward to coming home to play with my new little friends. On the way home, I spotted Mom down at the creek, so I walked over to see what she was doing.

Horrified at what I saw, I screamed as loud as I could. Mom was beating the puppies to death with a rock! She turned to see me as I ran off to the house in tears. She ran after me to explain why she had committed such a cruel act, but I didn't want to hear her voice. I was upset enough about losing

Eddie . . . and now this. I hated her for what she had done. I never thought a mother could do something like that.

I learned later that it was common in those days to kill an animal if you couldn't afford to feed it. Most of the coal miners and their families barely got by. The last thing they needed was another mouth—or seven!—to feed.

Mom tried and tried to explain it all to me, but I knew she wasn't sorry for what she'd done. She was only sorry I'd seen her, caught her in the act. I never got over seeing her down at the creek with those helpless little puppies in one hand and a large, bloody rock in the other.

* * *

We never had much in the way of new things, especially toys, but once Mom was called over to help a neighbor whose wife had suddenly taken ill. She was gone a couple days, and when she returned, she had presents for me and the other kids. They were simply wrapped in brown paper, and she said they were gifts from the man whose wife she was staying with. I opened mine, and inside was a beautiful porcelain doll I promptly named Sara. Sara became my constant companion. We ate together, slept together, and if I could have, I would have taken her to school with me.

One day, I came home from school and there was a strange man in the kitchen with Mom. I was angry when I saw him, since I knew Daddy was at work. I didn't know much about alcohol, but he looked like he'd been drinking. Mom was acting silly, too, and I saw him grab her backside.

When I left for school that morning, I'd placed Sara on the kitchen table in a makeshift cradle I'd created from an old box, but she was no longer there. The drunk, stumbling man had knocked Sara and her cradle to the floor.

Mom looked at me as I ran into the kitchen and grabbed the doll. There was an ugly crack between her eyes, smaller cracks splintering across her face, and a gaping hole in the back of her head. I held her to my chest and ran from the room in tears.

The man made no mention of it, except to say in his drunken slur, "Oops! Now, where were we?"

Mom giggled and said, "It's just an old doll. It doesn't mean anything."

But it did mean something to me. I loved Sara, and I had nothing to patch her with. So I carefully placed her on the piece of material I'd been using as a blanket and laid her on the bed to rest.

I was afraid to move her for fear of breaking her even more. Each day it became more painful to look at my beautiful Sara as she gazed up at me with those deep, dark eyes and the crack that had widened across her face. Some days I was certain I saw tears in her eyes. Was she in pain? I couldn't stand it any longer. I took Daddy's shovel, dug a hole under the wild grapevine on the hill, and buried my darling Sara.

When Mom found out what I'd done, she yelled at me. "How could you have done such a terrible thing? You buried something you claimed to love? It was just a stupid doll! What a horrible little girl you are!"

When Daddy came home that night, I was in bed but not asleep. I could hear her tell him what I'd done, though I could not hear his reply. The next day, he came out of the woods, and he made no mention of Sara. He walked over to where I was sitting and placed his hand on my shoulder. When I looked up at him, he smiled with a look of understanding in his eyes.

That's why I hated to tell him what I needed to tell him. I had not forgotten Mom's harsh words about Sara, so I told Daddy how Sara got broken in the first place.

He was quiet as he walked back into the woods.

* * *

Eventually, the house became too dangerous for us to live in as the ground beneath it eroded after the spring thaws. We moved into a four-room house down the street, a mansion in our minds. I remember walking down the road to the coal house to fetch coal to keep warm.

The coal was purchased from the company, and we would carry buckets to fill with our much-needed heat supply. When we didn't have the money to buy the coal, Jug and I would go down to the railroad tracks to pick up chunks of coal that had been tossed on the ground when the coal cars were parked on the tracks.

Other times we would climb up into the cars and fill our buckets. Sometimes as the trains crept by, men would see us and throw down pieces for us. We enjoyed chasing after them.

At this new house, I decided to make a little cemetery in the backyard where I would bury things. I guess my resentment toward Mom reared its ugly head, and I took her wedding ring and buried it.

I never told her and, to this day, no one ever knew. I grew up disliking her and felt that way until the very last year of her life. I will say this about her, though: I can’t recall her ever complaining or asking for help, even as she lay dying. Maybe she thought she didn't deserve it. At the time, I didn’t believe she did, either.

* * *

Mud slides and raging creeks were not the only thing we had to fear in those back woods of Appalachia.

It was while we were living in this house that Daddy and I would like to walk into town in the summer evenings and get ice cream. Although I was becoming a big girl, I was still Daddy's shadow and would follow him anywhere.

We had just left the company store, and I had a big scoop of strawberry ice cream on a cone. It looked so soft and refreshing; I couldn't wait to take a bite out of it.

On the way home, we saw a group of men in white sheets standing in front of my friend Hannah

Gershwin's house. In the yard, a tall cross was burning. I could feel the fear in Daddy's trembling hand as it gripped mine.

Suddenly, he jerked hard and my ball of strawberry ice cream toppled to the dirt. We ran through the back trees as quietly as we could so the men in white sheets couldn't see us. I had never seen Daddy scared, and it frightened me. He explained later that Indians were thought to be colored, and the Ku Klux Klan would make no distinction between the two.

Hannah was not Indian or colored, but Daddy explained that her family was Jewish and they were targeted as well. The next day, Hannah was not at school, and our teacher told us that she and her family had moved away during the night.

* * *

Daddy always did his best to make our dismal childhood a happy one. Every Christmas he made sleigh tracks in the snow and woke us kids up in the middle of the night to take a look. We'd run out into the snow to see Santa's tracks, proof that he had come to visit us the night before.

On the Fourth of July, all the families would get together at our house for a celebration. Aunts, uncles, cousins . . . they were all there. We'd get a five-gallon cardboard carton of ice cream and use big blocks of ice to keep it cold. We would chop up some ice and put it in galvanized washtubs and make pop in orange, cherry, and homemade root beer flavors. Usually, someone would bring a jar of moonshine, which was clear and looked like water. We'd have fireworks and play games like "greasy pig," where someone would grease a pig with lard and turn it loose in an enclosed area. Whoever caught it without losing his greasy grip would win a prize.

We also played horseshoes, ran three-legged sack races, and played a game called "pole." A six-foot pole was greased with lard, and if you climbed all the way to the top, you won a prize. If we got too hot, we damned up the creek and made a swimming hole, jumping in wearing just our underpants.

At Easter time, Daddy would color eggs with onion skins, red blood root, and purple pokeberries. Then he'd hide them in the house for us to find.

Despite our hard life, we had some fun times . . . thanks to Daddy.

* * *

I skipped kindergarten and went straight into first grade at six years old. Before I entered school, Daddy sat down with me and taught me how to read and count. We used a deck of cards to play a game similar to flash cards. By the time first grade started, I could count to one hundred backward and forward, and I could read the readers and primers.

After the first few weeks in school, the teachers could see I was more advanced than the other students, and I was tested for second grade. I passed. I then tested for the third and fourth grades and passed those as well. I passed the fifth grade test, too, but the school thought fifth grade children were too old for me to be around, so I was put back into the third grade.

Once a year, the school would have a fun day full of plays and other exciting activities. One of the games we played was called Fishing. We were given a wooden pole with a string tied to it and a safety pin on the end. We had to throw the line over an enclosed area where there was a poke—a paper bag—with a prize and candy inside. We had to pin the bag and reel it in. It was such fun.

One of the most popular candies was Sea Foam Fudge. I can still taste the sweetness of that fudge to this day.

Another popular game at the time was marbles. Everyone had their own collection and marble bag with their own steely marble, and you got to keep the marbles you won. Other games we enjoyed were hide-and-seek, ring-around-the-rosy, and dodgeball.

I could not get enough of plays and the theatre. I was chosen to play a sunflower, and I had a costume made out of crepe paper. I had to sing a song called "I'm a Little Sunflower." I was so proud of my costume and so happy that I had been chosen to be in a play. I loved to perform, and I was excited that everyone was going to see how pretty I looked.

Before I was set to go onstage, some snotty nose kid came up from behind me and grabbed at my costume. He ripped a gaping hole in the back of it, but the teacher was able to repair it just in time.

* * *

In spite of all this, I never lost sight of the

fact that I was different.

I don't know why, but Mom kept my blonde hair cut in a Dutch pageboy style. It was so embarrassing for me. My Aunt Veda, mom's sister, had married into money and became filthy rich and lived in a mansion. Every time she came to visit us she would say, "Why don't you put something in that child's hair?" I used to get so annoyed with her.

I never owned ribbons or fancy hair barrettes, so Aunt Veda took one of Jug's belts and tied it in a bow that flopped over like rabbit ears. All the children laughed at me, but in spite of their teasing, I wore it all day.

We could never afford nice things like fancy clothes, though Mom had grown up with such luxuries. I often wondered how she felt when Aunt Veda would visit.

She had made the decision not to disobey their father by marrying an Indian; she married well and kept her inheritance.

I wondered if Mom had any regrets about marrying Daddy, having us, and being forced to live in coal mining camps She did have one pair of beautiful, blue rayon hose—not nylons—with a big pink rose on each knee. I think it brought back memories of her time at Tarragon.

* * *

Sometimes I would hear or see things that other people didn't, and I was afraid to tell anyone. I had heard about people being sent away after hearing voices or seeing things that weren't really there, and I didn't want that to happen to me, so I told no one.

The first time I remember being afraid that someone would discover what had now become my secret, I was nine years old. I heard Mom and Daddy talk about our neighbor, Mr. Jackson, who had died from the bite of a black widow spider. The spider had made a nest under the seat of his outhouse, and as he sat down, it bit him on the buttocks. Two days later, he was dead. Since the wound was in an inconspicuous area, it had taken the coroner several days to determine the cause of death.

Three weeks after his death, Mom and I were returning home from the store when I saw Mr. Jackson approaching us from the opposite direction.

As I had been taught to respect my elders, I stepped aside to let him walk between us. Mom looked down at me and questioned why I'd made such a move. Without hesitation, I told her I had moved aside for Mr. Jackson, and I asked her why she hadn't spoken to him.

Later that night, I heard her telling Daddy about what had happened. I listened in fear of what his reaction might be. I was relieved when I heard him reassure her in his usual calm tone. "Maud, don't upset yourself. The first chance I get, I will talk to her."

Two days later, Daddy asked me to go squirrel hunting with him. I eagerly ran for my boots and joined him on the path to the woods. I loved those little trips with him. We never went far from home, and most of the time he made no attempt to kill an animal, even when the opportunity arose. I believed he enjoyed the seclusion more than the killing.

We came to a clearing, and Daddy asked me to join him on the carpet of green moss that grew around an old oak tree. For several moments, he didn't speak. I could sense him gathering his thoughts, searching for the proper approach to use when discussing Mom's fears with me. I waited in silence, concentrating on a leaf dancing in the breeze as it tried to hold onto its mother's branch.

Daddy sighed, placed his hand on mine, and began gently. "Virgie, I have suspected for some time that you have what your grandmother called 'the gift.' She had it, and so do I."

I changed my position and faced him, anxiously waiting for him to explain all the things that had happened to me that I'd been afraid to share with anyone.

"Virgie, I know there are times when you see people and hear things that others do not. I cannot explain why some of us have this gift and others do not. My mother always called us 'the chosen ones.' I have seen you when you are listening. Quite often I, too, heard the same voice. I also have seen people who have passed on. I do not know why they have returned. Often they are people I do not know. Sometimes they come to me at night when I am asleep. They wake me and talk to me of things I do not understand. Sometimes they sit on the side of my bed and talk of themselves. They tell me about their lives before their death, their loved ones, and their life after death. There are no messages, no earth-shattering confessions or revelations, just the feeling of loneliness and the need to talk to someone. Maybe that is what it's all about. They seek out one of us who is able and willing to listen. All I know is that it is a gift, and we must be proud to have been chosen. You must never abuse this privilege. You must never be afraid; they will never hurt you. My only warning is to be cautious. Do not speak of the gift to anyone. Perhaps someday there will be more understanding. But, for now, we must keep this as our secret. If you need to talk about it, please come to me at any time."

After our talk, I didn't question my ability. It wasn't until years later that I fully understood our conversation.

As time passed, I experienced some of the things Daddy had spoken of, and I understood what he had tried to explain to a nine-year-old who'd had no interest in being different. And I learned not to speak of my "happenings," as I called them, for the times that I did, I was misunderstood. I learned the hard way that Daddy was right in warning me to keep quiet about our secret.

* * *

There was still that other secret I was keeping: my mother's constant affair with Buster. They now had a child together, although Daddy was raising Opal as his own. One day while Daddy was at work, I couldn't find Mom. I went looking for her and found her naked in the garden with Buster, also naked, on top of her. I watched them for a few moments, not fully understanding their movements. Suddenly, she turned and saw me. She screamed and tried to cover herself as she got up. Buster scrambled to put on his pants and ran from the yard.

She ran into the house and locked herself in the bedroom. She stayed in there all day and when Daddy came home, there was no dinner and the house was quiet. He asked me where Mom was, and I pointed to the bedroom. He tried to open the door, but it wouldn't budge.

He went around to the side of the house and looked into the window. I heard him scream, "Maud, no!" At that, I heard the sound of breaking glass, and a shotgun blast echoed through the house.

Daddy ran out of the house with Mom in his arms. I thought she was dead. The neighbors ran to our home, and someone with a car put Mom and Daddy in the backseat and drove away.

Daddy came back later that night, but he was alone. He never said a word.

It was a long time till I saw my mother again.

Dicie

After Mom was taken away, I remember seeing Daddy walk down to the railroad tracks every day. One time I followed him, and I saw him sitting on the tracks, crying as though his heart was breaking.

Daddy had a hard time taking care of four young children when Mom was in the hospital, so he took us to live with his parents in Marytown. It was also closer to the hospital where Mom had been admitted.

I loved staying with my grandmother, and those days were some of the happiest I can remember. The house was always full of food and people, and I loved to hear her stories almost as much as I loved hearing Daddy's.

Listening to her, I could see why he was such a wonderful storyteller.

Mamaw's son, Cecil, a lineman with the electric company, lived in Pikeville, Kentucky. She told us once of the strange ritual he had every night. He would come home every evening and eat a whole scoop of sugar from her sugar bin. She got tired of him eating all her sugar, so one night she filled up the sugar bin with salt. "He never did it again," she said with a chuckle.

Another time he had complained to Dicie that her sandwiches tasted as dry as chicken feathers. The next day, he got sandwiches made with real chicken feathers. She certainly knew how to get her point across.

One night Mamaw took Jug and me to Uncle Cecil's house for a celebration. At first she was fine, but then Mamaw gasped, grabbed the doorframe, and collapsed. She was put in Cecil's car and driven to the hospital in Welch, West Virginia, one mile from Marytown. The doctor said she had suffered a stroke. She was paralyzed on one side and had trouble speaking. The only words she could mutter were, "Home, home . . ."

She was taken back to Marytown and put in her bed. One by one, she called all twelve of her children and many grandchildren to her side, and in her jumbled speech, she told each one something only they knew.

I was her oldest grandchild and the last one to be called in. I put my ear to her mouth and she said, "Listen." I listened as she rose up and looked at me. "Today is the day," she said. Those were the last words she ever spoke. She died in front of me.

It was 1938; she was fifty-five years old.

I watched as her daughters sat her up in a chair, dressed her in the green satin dress she had requested for burial, and fixed her floor-length black hair in the style she always wore.

After she died, I felt lost. I had adored her with the kind of love I wished I'd felt for my mother. She had made me feel loved and wanted, and now that she was gone I was afraid. But I had so many wonderful memories of her . . .

Like the time when she put up apples in the attic to dry, and I snuck up there and ate a whole bunch of them. I loved apples but didn't know dried apples would swell when they got wet. I was sick to my stomach all night long, but she never chastised me when I did something wrong. She felt I would learn my lesson on my own, and I did that time.

Or the times when I would help her shuck beans and cooked them after they dried. She taught me to make clabber, which I loved. We'd put milk in the window in the sunshine and let it ferment. Then we would mix cornbread into it. I guess it would be similar to today's yogurt.

At Christmas, she would always make up a salad of apples, oranges and mixed walnuts. She was ahead of her time, and would create new recipes and dishes to eat.

She used to pickle corn and green beans. She had shelves of jams and jellies with the wax on top—there were no lids—and brown paper tied with a string. She made the best peach butter and made her own apple butter and molasses.

Her house smelled like food all the time. She was also one of the first women in town to have her own washing machine.

Mamaw was an important part of my life. She'd brought me back to life as a stillborn baby, and she was in my range of vision when she left this earth.

After her death, we were sent back to her house in Marytown to live with our aunts while mom was still in the hospital and Daddy was working out of town.

One day while we were in school, a woman came to the classroom door. The teacher asked me to go with her, and I followed her out into the hallway. The woman was standing there with Jug, and I was concerned as to what was going on.

The teacher said, "This is Miss Turner. She is going to take you and your brother to live with someone. Go with her."

I protested. "No, we don't go with strangers. We have to go home after school. They'll be expecting us!"

"No, Virgie, they will not be expecting you and Wade after school. They know you won't be coming home." I was ten years old.

We were taken outside and put into a car. I screamed and fought and tried my best to stop them from taking us.

The woman told us she was with Social Services and was taking us to live with a new family. Now that my grandmother was gone, there was no one to take care of us.

What about my aunts? My Aunt Mabel who I adored? I later learned that she was the one who had us placed in foster care. I never forgave her.

I held onto Jug's little trembling hand. We were both scared to death.

I whispered, "If Mamaw was alive, this would never happen."

Foster Care
Hemphill, West Virginia

We were taken to a house of horrors in Hemphill, West Virginia, located between Capels and Welch in McDowell County. It was about an hour from the county seat of Welch and sat along the Tug Fork River.

The Hamiltons were terrible people. Franklin Hamilton had horrible bad breath. His wife, Geri, had teeth so brown and yellow they looked like a row of rotten corn kernels.

She was nice to the social workers' faces, and she would smile her dirty smile at them while they were in the house, but as soon as they left us in the Hamiltons' care, things changed. Jug and I were scared to death.

The house had two rooms and a porch, and a bed was put in the kitchen for me and Jug. She gave us a wash pan to bathe in, and I don't recall eating that first night we were there.

They had a dog named Queenie who was tied up and guarding the outhouse. The next morning, I got up and took care of Jug. The Hamiltons never even got out of bed.

The night before she had pointed down the holler and said, "The school is down there."

We walked to school and had to cross a highway to get there. We saw other children walking along a path and decided to follow them. We had to cross a swinging bridge with steps leading down to an open field. Once we got to school, we were overjoyed to see our little sister, Jewell, on the playground. We asked her where she'd been taken, and she pointed to a house down the road. It was owned by Olive Brown, Mamaw's sister-in-law, but Jug and I were not welcome there, so we could only see Jewell at school.

I wanted all of us to live together again. I wanted to know how Mom was doing and if she and Daddy even knew where we were.

Most of the time, the Hamiltons locked me and Jug out of the house. They were inside, drunk, and we couldn't wake them from their stupor. Sometimes it would be way after dark, and we still hadn't been let back inside.

Finally the door would open, and I had to make dinner for me and Jug. No one took care of us. They were either drunk or drinking all the time.

Once a month they would get their check for taking care of us, and they would cash it immediately and come home with bottles of whiskey.

On one occasion, Jug and I couldn't get into the house at all. It was late, and we were cold, tired, and hungry. We had nowhere to go, so we crawled into the doghouse with Queenie and went to sleep until morning.

I was afraid for us and did not want to end up at the Hamiltons' forever. I was also afraid that something would happen to me, and Jug would be left to face them on his own.

I was terrified of the hole in the outhouse after my experience of falling into one and landing in the "basement." Once I was using the outhouse and saw a long, white worm come out of me. I started to cry and thought I was dying. I wondered what would become of Jug if I died. The worm was nearly two feet long.

I never knew what a tapeworm was, but I was terrified and told no one. I just knew I was dying, and I was afraid to go to sleep at night.

After being locked outside all night, I was hell-bent on getting revenge. We couldn't get into the house to get our breakfast, and we were always hungry. This episode gave me the courage to speak out.

Once the Hamiltons woke up and let us into the house, it was well past noon and we had missed school. I marched into the house, and before she had a chance to know what hit her, I let Geri have it as she wiped the sleep from her eyes and the drool from her mouth.

"When that lady from Social Services gets here today, I'm gonna tell her everything that has been going on here. I'm gonna tell her that you and Mr. Hamilton stay drunk all day on the money she gives you to take care of us. I'll tell her how I cook all the meals, wash the dishes, and do all the housework, except on the day she comes." Once I had opened the dam, I couldn't close it.

"You are a dirty, old woman! You stink, and you haven't taken a bath since we got here. My mother took a bath every day, and she cooked and took care of us!"

"Your mother is a whore!" she yelled. "Why do you think you're here? She doesn't care anything about you and neither does your father. Don't you think he knew the welfare department was going to put you in a home? Don't give me this goody-goody talk about your mother. I have known your mother for years, and she has always been a slut. Looks like you're going to be the same way. So you shut your mouth, and get that worthless brother of yours dressed before Miss Wood gets here. I'll tell her that you're both sick, and I kept you home from school today. And if you say one word about what goes on here, I will beat you within an inch of your life and your brother, too. So you had better watch your step, dearie."

I didn't have time to reply. We heard a car pull up out front, and she ran to the window. "Get back in bed, both of you, and close your eyes and pretend to be asleep! She's brought someone else with her. Remember what I told you!"

We ran to our bed in the kitchen and lay down as instructed. I closed my eyes and listened to the sound of her voice change as she greeted Miss Wood. "Good morning, dearie, or should I say afternoon? How are you? I see you've brought a visitor with you. Come in and I'll fix you some coffee."

I could hear her in the kitchen making coffee for Miss Wood and her guest. I was surprised she even knew how to make a cup.

"We're not feeling too well here this afternoon," she continued. "Our dear children have come down with something, and I think Mr. Hamilton and I have caught whatever the children have. Please excuse the way the house looks. I just haven't felt like doing much today."

Miss Wood said she understood and not to worry. There was a lot of flux going around, and we had probably picked it up at school.

I peeked out from under my eyelashes to see if I could spot the other person who had come with Miss Wood.

Both women were seated at the kitchen table while Mrs. Hamilton prepared their coffee at the sink. I could only see the side of Miss Wood and the back of the other woman's head.

Since Mrs. Hamilton was paying no attention to us, I opened my eyes and studied the back of the other woman.

There was something familiar about her hair, and I realized it was the same auburn color as Mom's. As Mrs. Hamilton sat a cup of coffee before her, she said, "Thank you." There was something about her voice . . .

I sat up in bed, causing them to turn in my direction. The woman with the red hair walked over to the bed with her arms outstretched. I backed away from her, up against the wall, out of her reach. She let her arms fall to her sides and turned, looking at Miss Wood as if pleading for instructions.

"Virgie, this is your mother," Miss Wood said. I guess Mrs. Hamilton had lied to me when she said she knew my mother. From the look on her face I could tell she didn't recognize this woman either.

At the sound of the word "mother," Wade opened his eyes and stared at the woman who stood before us.

He was two years younger than me, and it had been almost a year since we'd seen her. Although she looked like our mother, her face was filled with lines I did not remember. Her eyes didn't smile as our mother's eyes had smiled.

I looked at this woman who resembled Mom, and I hurt inside. I hurt with a pain far greater than I'd felt earlier that morning.

I wanted to jump from the bed and run to her, hug and kiss her and comfort her. I wanted to tell her that everything would be all right. But too much time had passed. I no longer knew how to say "I love you," and I wasn't sure I could even say I liked her.

The pain ran too deep.

If only I had known then that she was different, that she didn't even remember us as her children. Someone had to tell her that Daddy and I and the little ones were her family.

She sat down on the side of the bed next to me and Wade. She looked around as if to gather strength from some unseen source. I could tell she didn't know us, but she wanted to. She was still a woman with a maternal instinct, and we were children in peril. She looked at us as though she wanted to love us but didn't know us well enough to show us that emotion.

I remembered back to another time when she would wake us up in the morning, before she was taken away. She would come in and put her hand on my leg and speak so softly it was as though she were not speaking at all.

Once I had gotten mad at her and she came

in to comfort me. She was loving to us then.

Then she would say, "Virgie do you remember when you were a little girl and you would wake up cross and irritable and out of sorts? Do you remember what I would tell you, something that my mother had taught me when I was a little girl? Do you remember?"

I nodded. "I remember some of it."

"Well, you would be so grumpy, and I would say to you, 'you feel like, you seem like, you don't know what you feel like, you seem like you do.' It never failed to get a smile from you. Do you remember?"

I nodded once again. I had remembered, and it took her months to teach me to say the riddle without mixing up the words.

I looked up at this woman who looked like Mom and said, "Do you know the riddle? You know, the one your mom told you when you were a little girl?"

She looked at me, then back at Miss Wood. She had no idea what I was talking about. I knew this could not be my mother.

She looked as though the thoughts were just on the edge of her mind, but she couldn't convey them. Yes, she might have known what I meant, in the back of her mind, but in the front it was gone.

I continued. "The one you used to tell me when I was grumpy, remember? My mom would remember. You are not my mother." Then I hid my face under the covers.

I felt her body rise from the bed, and I sensed her sadness from under the dirty sheet. She went back to the table, and soon afterward, the two women left.

When Miss Wood came back the next month, Mrs. Hamilton had cleaned us up beforehand and warned us to behave. "Be seen and not heard, and only answer when spoken to."

* * *

One day, I came home from school and saw the car in front of the Hamiltons' house. I knew it was not the day for Miss Wood's visit; it wasn't the first of the month. As I got closer, I could see someone talking to Mr. Hamilton and another lady.

It was the woman who resembled Mom. Jug ran to her and hugged her, and I ran into the woods. I hated her. She had let this happen to us and had abandoned us.

I watched them from the woods until she left. I finally came back, and Mrs. Hamilton screamed at me and called me a horrible child.

Mother had brought me a little shoebox that contained a new pair of shoes. They were the first pair of shoes I'd ever seen that had flaps on them. Jug wore his, but I wouldn't wear mine. They had come from *her*.

Days passed, and one day after school I decided to go home with Jewell. Olive Brown was a bitter, nasty woman who told me my brother and I were not welcome in her home. We had been "banned," she said.

The next month when Miss Wood came up the holler, I ran and hid from her, thinking Mom was with her again, but she was alone. I was hiding under the bed when they came in, and Mrs. Hamilton put on her fake smile and false charm.

I watched as they sat down at the kitchen table. When Miss Wood asked where Wade and I were, Mrs. Hamilton said, “Oh those sweet little dears! They’re around here somewhere.”

Miss Wood gazed around the kitchen and caught sight of the half-empty whiskey bottle Mrs. Hamilton had tried to hide behind the kitchen curtain. Cigarettes filled a filthy ashtray, and garbage had been piled up in the corner.

Seeing this was not the ideal place for us, she said, “Well, Mrs. Hamilton, we were going to wait until the children’s mother was well enough to care for them, but I think I’ll be taking them with me today. Could you please call on them to gather their things?”

Realizing that their monthly checks would now stop and their liquor supply would run out, Mrs. Hamilton challenged her decision to take us.

“Oh, are you sure you really want to do that? We think they’ll be better off here with us. We love them like they’re our own little ones. You can’t be too sure with that mother of theirs,” she whispered, “I understand she’s the town whore.”

Miss Wood looked uncomfortable and smiled politely. “Please gather the children, will you?”

Mrs. Hamilton, who knew she was no match for Social Services, slowly got up from the table and went to look for us. Miss Wood walked outside to her car. That was my chance to come out from under the bed. As I did, I caught a glimpse from the window as Miss Wood climbed into the car. That woman who looked like Mom was waiting for her.

As Mrs. Hamilton hollered for me, I realized I had to go with them. I went outside and stood next to Jug, who was holding a brown paper bag containing his meager belongings.

We were still wearing the same clothes we had arrived in almost a year before; only our shoes were different. I was wearing the new pair Mrs. Hamilton had bought me after the school sent home a note telling her it was too late in the fall to be coming to school without shoes. Jug wore the new shoes Mom had sent.

I still refused to wear that pair, and I left them at the Hamiltons'.

The drive back to Mamaw's was long and silent. Several times, Mom turned and looked back at us and smiled; however, I did not return it. I was not ready to accept this woman who had gone out of our lives so abruptly.

Where was she on the many nights Wade and I had cried ourselves to sleep or gone to bed hungry, or the nights we'd fallen asleep on the ground or in Queenie's doghouse? Where was she when we were too afraid to go into the house for fear of the Hamiltons' loud, drunken rages and things breaking as they fought?

Now she returns with a smile and blank look in her eyes, and I'm to forget everything? I would never forget, ever. Nor would I ever forgive her or Daddy for what they'd done to us.

It was late in the afternoon when we got back to Mamaw's. Daddy was standing on the front steps waiting for us. He ran to the car and yanked open the back door. Wade scrambled out, and I watched as they embraced. Then Daddy reached for me. I just looked at him and got out of the car on the opposite side.

I saw the look that passed between him and my mother. She touched him on the arm and said, "It will take time, Jesse. You should have seen the house they were living in and that horrible woman, Mrs. Hamilton. What a terrible-looking person she was." He placed his hand under her arm, helping her fragile body up the steps.

I avoided Mom and Daddy as much as possible. Each time one of them made a gesture of affection or tried to include me in their conversation, I left the room.

I felt a pain deep inside my stomach at the look of hurt on their faces, but I was not ready to forgive them for what they'd done to us.

I never trusted anyone again.

The Kidnapping

After we came home from foster care, Daddy took us back to live in Coalwood. I was afraid to get close to Mom and Daddy for fear of being taken away again. It was a long time till I could feel somewhat safe with them.

Although at times she didn't remember us, Mom had some feelings of compassion toward us and was still a kind woman. It must have been hell for her, as it was for us, when she was released and given to a stranger and his children and told we were her family.

I wish I had known.

I was told the neighbors down the street, the Huffmans, had been watching the baby while Mom was ill. Once Mom was home, Daddy told me to go down there and get Opal so we could all be a family again.

The house had a porch that wrapped all the way around it. I stood there and knocked on the door. When I got no response, I peered in the window. The house was empty.

Suddenly, a man in the next yard hollered out, "Hey, you looking for Huffman? They moved a couple weeks ago."

"Well, where is my sister?"

The man look confused. "I don't know nothin' about your sister, but they had a baby with them if that helps."

I couldn't believe what my little ears were hearing. I ran home and told Daddy.

Daddy, who was a quiet and gentle man, said it would be all right, that they must have left a note of some kind. No one would just take their baby like that. Mom was beside herself with worry and grief as Daddy tried to reassure her that they would find Opal. "Don't worry, Maud, they'll get in touch with us, you'll see. It will be all right."

But they never did.

Mom had a crying spell every day and would lock herself in her room for hours on end. Once I found a little Easter bonnet that belonged to Opal, and Mom saw me with it. She grabbed it from my hand, ran into her bedroom, and slammed the door. I heard the key turn in the lock.

I went outside to wait for Daddy to come home, and I told him about Mom and the bonnet. Daddy went inside the house to find her. I was scared and ran back inside since the last time Mom had locked herself in the bedroom, she'd been taken away.

The bedroom door was locked, and Daddy, who was not a big man, tried to break it down. He kicked at it until it flew open. Mom was sitting in the corner of the room on the other side of the bed with a loaded shotgun across her lap.

Daddy told me to go outside, but I didn't listen. I watched as he lifted her and gently put her on the bed. She said she tried to shoot the gun to end her pain, but it wouldn't go off. The safety had been on, and she didn't know how to unlock it.

I didn't understand that she had concern for Opal but not much for us. She didn't even seem to know us, but she got that upset about the missing baby? Another reason to resent her and her lover's child.

I hated Opal and was secretly glad she was gone. Although she was only twenty-six-months-old, she was mean–spirited, and I don't even remember her being born. I didn't like taking care of her; however, I was the oldest, and Opal became my responsibility. It felt natural for me to dislike her, and I think it was because I knew she wasn't Daddy's baby.

Shortly after her birth, Mom said she had felt so guilty about the baby not being Daddy's that once when she was giving her a bath, she had the urge to push her under the water and drown her.

At some point, she told Mrs. Huffman about her feelings, and, visibly concerned for the baby's welfare, the woman decided the baby would be better off with her and Mr. Huffman. So while Mom was in the hospital, they took her.

It took a few years, but Mom and Daddy tracked them down in Ohio. Daddy contacted them, and Mom and Jewell went to visit Opal. The Huffmans said they felt Mom had been through enough, and Opal would be better off with them. Why no charges were ever filed against them, I don't know. I guess times were different then.

By now, she had grown into a little girl who favored Mom with her creamy complexion and auburn hair. But she didn't know her mother or her sister. This broke Mom's heart, and the guilt crept back inside her.

When Mrs. Huffman passed away, Mom was notified and went to Ohio. At the funeral she turned to Mr. Huffman and said, “Well, Edgar, I might as well take Opal home with me now.”

At that, Mr. Huffman replied, “Maud, would you take the last thing I’ve got in the world?”

After that, Mom never saw her again.

It wasn’t until Opal was twenty-nine years old that Jewell found her through her Army records.

* * *

When Mom came home from the hospital, she no longer baked or sang to us, and the loving feeling she always showered us with was gone. She no longer tucked us in at night or told us stories to help us fall asleep.

I became the mother and was now in charge of the other children and the household. I kept hoping each day that she would revert back to being our mother again. Although we had our problems, I missed the mother I’d known and couldn’t understand why she had gone into the hospital as one woman and came back another.

Why didn’t someone tell me?

We were poor, and although I tried hard to fit in with the other children, I was different and made to feel like an outcast.

There was a woman in town named Mrs. Fox who had a daughter named Ruth, and she wouldn’t let her play with me.

Mrs. Fox belonged to a garden club and raised dahlias, and her husband was a mining engineer. They would not associate with the miners or their families; it was beneath them.

One day I overheard her tell Ruth, “I don't want you playing with her. She is a dirty little girl who always has a runny nose. She probably has lice.”

I did not have lice. Mom was a clean woman and always made us take a bath.

Ruth’s mother would only dress Ruth in clothes that made her resemble Shirley Temple. One day, Ruth had a birthday party, and I wanted so badly to be invited but I wasn't. Her mother wouldn't allow her to invite me.

I watched in sadness as all the little girls from the wealthy part of town walked over to her house, dressed up in their pretty party dresses. Ruth saw me outside and told me if I went around to the back of the house she would bring me a piece of cake.

As I made my way around to the back of the house, Ruth came out and slipped me a piece of cake through the fence.

Suddenly, her mother grabbed Ruth by the arm and the cake fell to the ground. Ruth was led back inside with the other children. I just stood there and looked at the piece of cake all covered in dirt. Mrs. Fox always treated us like trash.

Another little girl, Helen Blankenship, was a thorn in my side. She was a big girl who seemed to tower over my petite frame. She would wait for me after school every day and beat me up on the way home. She would see me coming and with a running leap, she’d hit me in the back with her closed fist.

One day as I made my way to the coal house

to fill up my bucket, I stepped up onto the bridge, and I could see her standing there. The bridge was in the middle of two sets of steps, and Helen was standing at the top of the steps with a rock in her hand. She threw the rock at me and ran away. I momentarily lost my breath and fell backward as the rock hit the middle of my chest.

As I fell, my coal bucket cut me on the ankle. I couldn't breathe. Someone came over and helped me to my feet, though I'm not sure who it was.

Helen's father made her come to my house and apologize. He told us she had lost her mother a few months before, and she was still grieving and didn't know how to deal with her loss. But loss or not, I was sick and tired of her beatings. I, too, had had many losses in my short life, but I didn't resort to hitting innocent people with large rocks.

Although her apology seemed sincere in front of her father, her abuse did not stop. One day as we were walking home from school, I could feel her coming up behind me. I whipped around and pushed her as hard as I could with both hands.

When she fell onto the sidewalk, I jumped on her and started hitting her as hard as I could. When Daddy found out, he didn't punish me. He had always told me, "Don't ever start a fight, but don't walk away from one, either. You finish it." She never bothered me again.

* * *

Once a month, the nurses at school would

come around to check us for various ailments and body lice. Some of the children were told they needed to have their tonsils taken out, and I and one of the other little girls from my grade were among them. The other girl was admitted to Welch Hospital, where she died during surgery. After that, Daddy refused to let me have the surgery.

In those days, some women were known as a “hired girl,” a housekeeper and mother's helper of sorts for women who could afford them.

One such girl was a twenty-year-old named Hester, and she and I became friends. Hester's boyfriend, Joe, had a car with a rumble seat, and I loved to ride in it with them.

Welch had the closest movie theater, and when Hester and Joe invited me to go with them one night, Daddy said no. He never let me go out at night. He’d had one of his “feelings” and tried to convince the couple to stay home as well. I cried and cried because at that time, I didn’t want him to be different. Plus, I had never seen a movie before, and I wanted to ride in the rumble seat again.

The next day, I didn‘t see Hester as planned. Both she and Joe had been killed the night before as they left the theatre.

Daddy had always had a keen sense of knowing, and I never questioned him again after that.

Caretta, West Virginia

After Opal went away, we moved to Caretta, West Virginia. The doctor had suggested to Daddy that we move again after the gun incident and the kidnapping and said Mom should have another baby as soon as possible.

Daddy got a job in the mines. The town was nice with a company store and a boardinghouse.

Our house was in the holler up from the town of Caretta in a little area known as Greasy Creek. The mines were located on the left, two to three miles up the road. Opposite the mines was the road where we lived. The school was nice and about four miles away.

Caretta was the nicest place we'd ever lived. Most of the towns we'd lived in had been coal mining camps, but Caretta was more like a hamlet. The town was owned first by The Virginia Pocahontas Coal Company, then by the Carter Coal Company, and the final operators were Consolidation Coal.

Whoever owned the mines determined the type and condition of the houses the miners and their families lived in. Some housing in other coal camps had no water or electricity, but Daddy made sure that, wherever we lived, we did not go without these necessities.

The street in Caretta wasn't paved, but it was kept up; there were no potholes. All the houses were the same size—four rooms and a porch on front and back—and there was a commode that you had to reach upward to flush, but at least it was inside. There was board fencing around each house, and all the yards were well kept and nice. I used to think whoever owned those mines really cared about their miners.

I would hear Daddy talk about a man he greatly admired named John Lewis, who served as president of the United Mine Workers of America. Daddy said he was an important man in the coal mining business and was responsible for the miners making better wages.

He said that since the country was so dependent on the use of coal, and the safety of the miners was always in question, he helped to organize a five-month strike to ensure better wages and safer conditions. Since he was the man who got Daddy more money and made him safer in the mines, next to Daddy, he was my hero.

There were two company stores in Caretta, one by the mines and one by the houses. The company stores were not divided by race. The coloreds, the Spanish, the Italians, and the Polish all got along. Men of all races and nationalities played cards together, and there was no prejudice between them.

The women would serve food as the men played. The whites would go into the colored section of town, but the coloreds never ventured into the white part.

I never could understand why there were two different schools—one for the white children and one for the coloreds—since all the children walked the same road and their parents got along.

The children had no prejudice against one another either. We would all get together and play. One game we all loved was to curl up inside a tire, which were wider in those days, and get pushed down Turkey Knob, a hill in the colored section.

At the end of the hill there was a bridge over a creek, and we put a three-foot-wide board over it to get across. The goal was to roll the tire over the board without the kid inside falling into the creek.

* * *

Each time we moved into a different town we would advance financially, and our personal lives would always improve, too. In Caretta we had coal heat, a fireplace, a cookstove, and indoor plumbing. If we were lucky, we would get one pair of shoes a year when school started.

Daddy's job at the mines improved, too. The wages were better, and for the first time we were able to buy furniture.

Daddy bought a green couch, maroon draperies, a chair, and a bed for him and Mom. We kids got a bed and a chest of drawers, but since the room was shared by everyone, there didn't seem to be any room left for the new furniture. We also got a new table and chairs for the kitchen, which had those wooden floors Mom insisted on bleaching white with lye.

And no matter what, we always had the cloth napkins Mom brought with her from Tarragon. Before she got ill, Mom said that no matter how poor we were, cloth napkins would make us feel rich . . . and she was right. All the goods came from The May Company, a furniture company in town.

Mom, who seemed to be adjusting, made sure we had a bath every night. Sometimes she would heat water on the stove to use as each child came out of the big galvanized washtub that served as our bathtub.

We used Octagon soap that we used on clothes when we ran out of Rinso, but it smelled terrible.

I had a friend in Caretta named Maxine Boyd. Her father was not a coal miner, but her mother was a teacher at our school. Each time I went over to her house, her mother was doing the laundry, and we would laugh at her father's underwear because of the "skid marks" all along the back of them.

Mrs. Boyd was a frail, quiet woman who gave the impression that she might faint at any given moment. I don't think she ever really approved of my friendship with her daughter and was probably only nice to me because Maxi had asked her to be.

Since Mrs. Boyd was a teacher, on cold mornings she would let me and Maxi ride to school with her. On mornings when she left early, we would walk the four miles together.

We didn't have hats or gloves, and at that time girls did not wear long pants, so the cold weather was brutal on our bare legs. On winter mornings, we would arrive at school so cold that the moisture in our nostrils was frozen. Our hands and feet were so cold that it seemed like hours before they would function properly.

I always enjoyed playing at Maxi's house, except for one thing: a huge, oval, heavily-framed picture Mrs. Boyd had hanging in their living room. It had a lot of strange symbols, including a large eye that seemed to follow and watch me no matter what part of the room I was in. It really bothered me. I always wondered where it came from, but I was too scared to ask. With my vivid imagination, I always imagined that she was involved in something dark and mysterious, but I never knew for sure.

There was a creek at the back of our house, and Maxi and I would look for crawfish there. We'd make furniture out of flat rocks and use moss as the upholstery. We used to pick blackberries in late summer, and we would gather them up and sell them for ten cents a basket along the road in front of our house. We'd then take our earnings and wait for the candy man to come around once a week. We'd each buy a piece of candy. Bit-O-Honey, coconut stamps, and Necco Wafers were a special treat.

On rainy days, we would play under the house, where we took comfort in our childhood solitude. We would usually play under Maxine's house, since the porch was up higher and gave us more room to play. We would use a sheet to divide the rooms of our pretend house, and we would pair off into couples.

Nine-year-old Jug would come along and play with us; however, once I saw him playing house with Maxine as his wife, and he was really playing house. My nine-year-old brother was actually having sex with her!

* * *

In 1939 or '40, the miners went on strike. They were trying to unionize, but the mine owners didn't want them to. "Scab" labor was brought in to replace the men who refused to work without the protection of a union, and some of the scab workers were killed, beaten to death with baseball bats or shot.

Daddy was a peace-loving man and wanted no part of the violence, so he found work out of town and decided to wait it out.

Each payday, money was taken out for miners' dues, used to buy food to feed the miners' families whenever they went on strike. Every April, the miners went on strike, and Daddy headed out of town again to find work.

If you didn't work, you couldn't pay your rent and were evicted from your home. If the wife had no husband at home to pay the rent, the family had to leave.

While Daddy was gone, the company truck would bring supplies to the families, but it was only a one-time trip. They would bring rice, potatoes, lard, salt—no pepper—yeast, flour, baking powder, and canned milk. If you were lucky, you might get some dried peaches before they ran out. The food had to last the duration of the strike.

One day, a truck drove up out front. Two men got out and came into the yard. One, carrying a hammer and nails, walked onto the porch and nailed a huge, white sign to our front door. I followed the other man to the back of the house where he removed two thin, silver wires with small round cylinders on the end from his back pocket. He placed them on the wires of the electric fuse box and then used his pliers to twist the wire together so they couldn't be removed without breaking them.

He had cut off our electricity.

I ran around to the front of the house to read the sign on the front door. In red letters, big enough that anyone passing by could read them, was one word: *Vacate!* I couldn't read all the words under that one, but I knew what the sign meant. We would have to move out of our house.

It also meant that someone had not paid the rent.

Since Mom was entertaining every man in town, I thought maybe she'd missed these two. If she'd been nice to them, maybe we wouldn't have to move. I sat down on the steps and wondered where we were going to go.

Daddy was out of town working, and I was afraid he wouldn't be able to find us if we moved.

Mom had given birth to a son, Billy Ray, at the Welch Hospital two days before Christmas in 1938, and she was left with four children to raise on a miner's pay. Daddy, the miner, was still out of town.

A few days later, my Uncle Chester—he really wasn't an uncle, but I was told to call him that—came by and told us he had been sent over to move us.

I did not like him. He didn't look at me as he talked to Mom, and I watched him as he told her we would have to leave that day because someone else was going to be moving in.

Uncle Chester was employed by the company as a forest ranger. Although I didn't like him, he was handsome and stood well over six feet tall. He looked stylish in his light tan uniform with dark brown boots that laced all the way up to his knees.

Sometimes he did other jobs, like moving people who the company had instructed him to relocate. I heard Mom tell him that we had no place to go, and no, she didn't know were Daddy was. She also asked him if he could give her till the end of the week to find something. I hated to hear the pleading in her voice.

I wondered if the rumors I had heard about him and Mom were true, that Uncle Chester had fathered Billy Ray. He had stayed with us for several months before he found work, but with Mom's reputation, she probably didn't even know who the father was.

Uncle Chester found us a place to live next to a boardinghouse. He brought his company truck to help us move, but The May Company came and repossessed all of our beautiful furniture, since we couldn't pay for it with Daddy gone.

Mom and the baby shared a cot in the corner of the room. We had to sleep on the floor in front of a fireplace to keep warm since we had no electricity, and Mom, who was always a nervous woman, was afraid we would "cook our brains" by being too close to the heat. During thunderstorms, she would make us all sit in the middle of the room, and we weren't allowed to get near anything metal.

We eventually ran out of coal, since we had no money to buy any. Jug and I would walk along the tracks and pick up what we could, but we'd end up with only about half a bucket, which didn't last very long.

One night, I had a dream about the baby. In it I saw two white doves holding a banner that read *Billy Ray, May 4, 1939.* I should have known not to tell Mom about the dream, knowing how superstitious she was, but I did anyway.

"Something is going to happen to Billy Ray," I said.

She got very upset with me. "Don't tell me things like that. I don't want to hear it."

About a month later, almost to the day, Mom noticed something was wrong with Billy Ray. His eyes rolled back in his head, and he began choking and shaking.

I heard her say, "Something is wrong with the baby; he's acting funny." After two or three similar episodes, Mom fixed him a bottle. He drank three ounces, and she thought he would be okay. But later on that night, he vomited up the milk, and a rusty-colored fluid came out of his mouth and nose. He needed a doctor.

It was pitch-black outside because the electricity had been cut off in so many of the houses. Mom was worried about the baby, but she was also worried about me going out alone at night that she made me wait until morning. I wonder now if it would have made a difference if I'd been brave enough to go sooner.

At daybreak, I ran four miles to the doctor's house, passing an old, haunted Indian cave. When I finally reached the house, the doctor's wife answered the door.

I was hoping the doctor would come right away and give me a ride back into town, but the wife kept saying, "Go on home, and he'll be there when he can." I kept insisting that Billy Ray was deathly sick, and we needed help right away, but she practically shoved me out the door.

It was almost noon when the doctor finally came. Mom was on the cot under the window with the baby. The brown fluid coming out of Billy Ray caused a horrible smell in the room. The doctor leaned over Mom, opened the window, and said, "Good fresh air never hurt anyone."

While he was standing there talking to Mom, Billy Ray died. The doctor didn't tell us anything about the way he died, but the death certificate said pneumonia. It was May 4, 1939.

The doctor told us someone would come by and pick up the body, and he left Billy Ray on the cot with Mom. Not too long after, a car pulled up, and a man with a suitcase in his hand got out, walked up to the front door, and, opened it without knocking. He didn't say a word.

When he opened the suitcase, I noticed it didn't have a liner. He put Billy Ray inside, and as he lifted it up, we heard a loud thud as Billy Ray's lifeless little body fell to the bottom of the suitcase.

I grabbed the man by the leg and beat on him for mistreating my little brother that way.

Mom sat by the window all day. We were hungry, but we didn't have enough potatoes to feed all of us, so I made a pile of them and cooked them with water over the fireplace. Mom didn't eat.

The next day, a man came over with a beautiful white casket with satin lining. Billy Ray was inside in a little white gown.

A stand was placed in the room, and the man sat the casket on it. Mom pulled up a chair and sat by the casket all day and night, her head resting on top of it.

The neighbors brought food over; it seemed like a banquet to me. I felt guilty about Billy Ray dying. I hadn't wanted another kid to take care of, since every baby that came along ended up being my responsibility. I wrote a song for him after he died, and in it I told him I was sorry for all the things I'd thought and said about him.

I waited and waited on the front steps, hoping and praying that Daddy would find us and come home.

All of a sudden, I looked up and saw Daddy coming around the corner, his hands full of packages. I couldn't believe it after all this time. I was glad someone had told him where we'd moved. He dropped the packages as I ran into his arms.

Daddy saw all the neighbors in the yard and said, "Hey girl, what's going on?" Before I could answer, some of the neighbors who were standing at the gate came over and offered their condolences to him. He ran into the house and saw the tiny casket on the stand.

He'd bought a gift for Billy Ray, a white satin pillow beautifully embroidered with the words Our Darling.

He gently lifted Billy Ray's head and put the pillow underneath it. As his shadow, I followed him to the back porch, and he sat down and began to cry. He cried so hard his shoulders shook. I had never seen him cry like that before or ever again.

Mom was in another world. Already a stranger to us, she'd been trying to adjust to her new role as wife and mother, but Billy Ray's death really set her back. Daddy, too, was broken. Every day that passed, I prayed that the mother I knew would return and love us again.

But after losing Billy Ray, her world—and ours—was never the same.

* * *

Mom's flirtations with other men became more and more evident to Daddy, whose pride could not allow him to take anymore.

After the baby's death, she began flirting with some of the men who lived next door at the boardinghouse, and Daddy soon found us another place to live in the same town. I wondered how long it would take him to eventually run out of places to go if he had to move us every time Mom slept with a neighbor.

After Daddy went back to work, I noticed that we suddenly had food in the house. I wasn't complaining, but as a hungry and curious child, I wanted to know why we went from being hungry and poor one day to having enough food to eat the next. It became clear to me that Mom was getting money from other men, and she wasn't doing their laundry to earn it.

It was common in some coal mining camps for women to find side work in prostitution in order to feed their starving brood. But my own mother? Hadn't she caused Daddy enough pain? But I found that many men accepted the fact that their women sold their bodies to other men for money.

When Daddy moved us to Dantown, which was a suburb of Caretta, we lived in the boardinghouse in town.

Daddy starting hiding his money from working in the mines, and for whatever reason, Mom did what she did. It seemed to be the normal way of life there.

I suppose the men who approved of this way of life for their women looked at all females in that manner, as willing to lay down for any man, but I was not one of them.

Mom always told us to walk on the sidewalk when we went into town, but there was a little girl named Elizabeth who used to pick on me. She was an odd girl who was born without ears, just little holes on the side of her head. "Don't you ever wash your hair?" she would say.

One day I was in town and saw her coming toward me, so I got off the sidewalk and took a path that led down to the railroad tracks, which ran parallel to the sidewalk in town. Down by the tracks was the roundhouse. I ran as far as I could and stopped when I saw a coal car on the pathway. I got scared as I realized I was far from home, so I began to walk faster.

Suddenly I heard a man say, "Little girl, come here."

I heard footsteps behind me as the gravel crunched beneath his feet. I finally turned around and saw a man standing there with his pants down around his knees, shaking his penis at me. I just remember it was red and disgusting, and he chased me when I ran.

I got away, and I never told anyone. I didn't think anyone would care.

After a while, Mom stopped trying to hide her affairs from me. She began seeing a man I knew only as Russell. Before she went out, she told me to lock the front door but keep the bedroom window unlocked.

That way, she could sneak in and out of the house but still keep her children protected behind a locked door.

One night, Daddy came home from work unexpectedly and Mom was out with her lover, Russell. Daddy asked me where she was, and I didn't answer him, but he knew. Scared, I went into the kitchen and hid the butcher knife and then ran into my room.

Although Daddy was Cherokee and not a violent man, he was still a man who had his pride, and Mom kept walking over it time and time again.

Eventually, she came home and climbed in through the bedroom window. Daddy was sitting on the bed. I heard the window slide open, followed by a loud thud. I ran into their room. Daddy had hit Mom in the face as she came in through the window, and she'd fallen back onto the ground outside. He opened the door, and she came back inside, crying.

I had never seen Daddy violent before or after that, but I felt Mom deserved it.

There was no talking, no fighting. He just forgave her like he always did, no matter what. I guess on that night he'd just had enough.

Later, I heard them having sex in their bedroom.

After this incident, I hoped Mom would calm her sexual ways with men, but the opposite happened. She began to openly flaunt herself as a prostitute. She explained it away by saying all the wives did it for extra money. It was either wash and iron clothes for others, clean houses, or sleep with men for money.

Since she was already sleeping with men other than my father, she said she might as well make money doing it.

* * *

There was a tall, gangly boy in the area named Tom, who was about fourteen, gentle, and severely retarded. He used to wrap his feet in rags because he had no shoes.

The rags would be bloody from the wear and tear he put on his feet. Mom felt sorry for him and always fixed him a hot meal and would replace his rag-shoes with whatever scrap material she could find. He was always welcome in our home, and Mom worried about him all the time. She said it wouldn't surprise her if something happened to Tom one day, because he stumbled and fell frequently due to his mental state. He was actually pitiful to watch.

One day when he was at the house, I looked at him, and I actually saw him dead. He was lying down and looked like he was asleep, but I knew he was dead.

When I told Mom, she said she didn't want to hear it. But like Daddy had told me, there was nothing I could do to change my visions, so I was not afraid and accepted the fact that Tom would soon be dead.

A few days later, a delivery truck from the furniture store pulled up out front. Daddy had gotten us a washing machine on credit, the first one we ever owned. It was a ringer washing machine, and it came with twenty-five boxes of Rinso washing powder. We were so happy with the added bonus.

As the truck pulled out after the delivery, Tom walked out our front gate and stumbled right into the path of the oncoming truck. He was knocked down, run over, and killed right in front of us.

Sometimes my visions would come at night in the form of dreams. One such dream was about our neighbor, Balthazar Baranowski, who was the head of a Polish family who lived across the street. He was a loud, but charming, heavyset man who had a wonderful family. They were the nicest people you could ever meet. That is why my dream was so disturbing to me.

In the dream, I saw Mr. Baranowski killing someone. It terrified me, since there was no way that kind, sweet man was capable of anything so horrible. Although I thought it was ridiculous, and I didn't tell anyone, I could not get that vision of him out of my mind.

A few days later, Daddy came home from the mines, and he was quite upset. In those days, parents did not consult or confide in their children about their problems; however, our house was so small, I could usually overhear everything being said between them.

Daddy said a man was found dead in the mines, killed with a pickax that had been embedded in his head. Whoever did it, Daddy said, left behind his copper tags. The tags were a form of identification for the miners, containing a specific number that had been assigned to each man.

The tags were worn on the belt, and their purpose was not only for identification, but they were needed in order to pick up script, the company store money.

Well, the tags found by the dead man's body belonged to Mr. Baranowski, who was charged with murder, found guilty, and convicted to life in prison.

* * *

Back in the 1930s and '40s, it was not uncommon to have door-to-door salesman make their calls and be invited in for dinner. In some cases, they were even invited to spend the night.

There was a man named Vinton who made a living retreading tires. The retread man, as we called him, stopped by the house one day looking pale and sickly. I could tell something was wrong with him. When he started to pass out, I hollered for Mom, and we got him inside, put him on the bed, and gave him a hot drink. He told us he was suffering with pneumonia, and Mom said he could stay with us until he was feeling better.

This worried me, since I knew Mom's reputation with men, but in his condition, I would've been surprised if he could lay carpet, let alone Mom.

After a few days, Mom and Daddy went into nearby War, West Virginia, to buy groceries. Daddy had been complaining that the company store was charging too much for their items, so he went into War to buy food.

Back then, Daddy and the other miners used company script to pay for their necessities. With each script, you were charged a fee in order to have the script converted into paper money. For example, if the script note was for ten dollars, you might be charged one dollar for the conversion.

Daddy said that since we were cash poor, the company store, which was owned by the coal company, would issue script and could charge outrageous fees for goods. Since our area was so remote, the workers had little choice but to purchase items at the company store, making the workers completely dependent on the company, which enforced employee loyalty. Many people didn't own a car and didn't want to walk into War, so they paid the high prices at the store.

While they were at the store, I was left in charge of taking care of Vinton. I was eleven years old. I walked into his room to check on him, and he had my six-year-old sister, Jewell, on top of his naked body. He had her slightly underneath the covers as he rubbed her up and down on himself. I had just come inside after gathering coal and still had the bucket in my hands.

I threw that coal bucket down, grabbed Jewell—who was not wearing any underpants—put her down on the floor, and told her to go outside and play. Vinton pulled the covers up over his face, and I jumped on top of him, straddled him, and began beating on his face and penis with the coal shovel. He was completely naked, and he was trying to cover himself, but I continued to beat him until the shovel broke.

If the shovel had not broken, I would have killed him. I wish I had. For a man with pneumonia, he sure jumped out of bed fast, grabbed his bags and left.

When Mom and Daddy came home, I told them he was gone. I never told them what had happened. Sadly, this kind of behavior was all too common. Although I was a feisty little thing, I was not immune to such lewd conduct.

Daddy had a friend we called Uncle Mike. He liked to pick me up and sit me on his shoulders and wiggle his finger under my dress and into my privates. I never told anyone.

Another time, my Aunt Elizabeth, one of Daddy's sisters, became pregnant. She was married to Howard, a man I didn't really care for. I was sent to their house to help her. They only had two rooms and a front porch, and the only place for me to sleep was at the foot of their bed.

One night, Howard put his foot up under my nightgown and molested me. I got up and went out front and slept in a chair.

I never told Aunt Elizabeth, though she tried to make a bed for me on the floor. After trying to stave off Howard's advances, I'd had enough. I only stayed a couple days and returned home.

Mom wanted to know why I didn't stay longer when Elizabeth needed my help, but I never told her or anyone. I was not much into confiding in people.

After the foster care incident, I learned not to trust.

Pikeville, Kentucky

When I was twelve years old, Daddy got a job as an inspector at the Pepsi-Cola plant in Pikeville, Kentucky. His job was to sit in front of a large magnifying glass and inspect the bottles as they came through on the conveyor belt. He made eleven dollars a day. We thought we were rich.

He opened an account at the local grocery store, which he had never done before, because Daddy was too proud to owe anyone anything. But we had nowhere to stay except my Uncle Cecil and Aunt Maxi's place until we found a place of our own, and he wanted to put some money away for us.

Eventually, a house down the street became vacant, and we were able to rent it and move in. The house had two long rooms and rested along a hillside.

We moved in during the night without much light or inspection. In the light of day, we noticed that the windows had bars on them. Daddy had heard stories that an elderly man who lived there before us had married a teenage girl and had bars put on the windows to keep her a prisoner.

There were only four windows in the whole place, and they were all located on one side of the house; the other side was actually built into the hillside. There were two heavy doors on each end of the house.

In the daylight, Wade, Jewell and I went exploring. Over the knoll, we found an old cemetery. I didn't want to live near a boneyard. Mom was superstitious, so I was hoping she would never find out about it. When she did, she had a fit. She said she didn't want us to live there, but we had nowhere else to go.

Living in that creepy house, I heard things I didn't think anyone else could hear, and I was afraid all the time. Then I remembered what Daddy told me about "the gift" and how I should keep it a secret.

I always did the mealtime dishes, and when I was finished, I would throw the dirty water onto the ground outside the back door. Once the water soaked down, the dirt would turn a red, rusty color. I never thought much of it until I heard the story behind the strange house.

Seems the old man who lived there thought his young wife was cheating on him. He came home one night to find a young man there, who panicked when he saw the husband come through the door. The old man picked up a shotgun and shot the boy as he tried to run. He bled to death outside the back door, and the ground was forever tinted red from the blood.

After hearing that, Mom never walked through that back door again.

Daddy would work nights, but he kept a shotgun in the bedroom for Mom to use in case of trouble. I never understood that, since she was not to be trusted around guns after the last two incidents.

Mom was a scared, nervous woman who instilled fear in us without even realizing it. Since she was so afraid in that house, I had to sleep in bed with her until Daddy came home.

The house was wallpapered with pages from old magazines. Daddy and I would hear noises in the house: a knife slitting paper, someone pounding on the doors, and once we thought we heard a dog shaking off water. There was nothing out there.

During those times, Daddy and I would look at each other, but no words were ever spoken.

One time, Mom and Daddy went to the store and left me and the little ones at home. We were playing under the front porch when we heard someone walking inside the house. Mom always wore high heels, and it sounded like her; however, when I went upstairs to see her, no one was there.

Another night, while Daddy was at work, Mom woke me up from a sound sleep. "I think someone is in the corner. Look over there," she whispered.

"I don't see anything," I said, though I was too scared to look and had my eyes closed tight.

I grabbed the shotgun and yelled into the darkness, "We have a gun!" I pulled the trigger, and the gun went off, the blast knocking me off my feet. There was a huge hole in the middle of the floor.

After that, Daddy found another place for us to live. The house was a store front in town, across from the Pepsi-Cola plant, near the railroad tracks on Hellier Street. It had two rooms for us downstairs; the upstairs had a bathroom and several other rooms. There was another bath off the kitchen. Several people lived there as well.

We later learned that the house we were living in was a house of ill repute—in laymen's terms, a whorehouse.

A woman by the name of Rosie Blackburn was the madam, and she had only two girls working there for her, Zelda and Velvet. The youngest, Zelda, actually went to school with me, and she would come to school with her wrists covered in bruises she was constantly trying to cover up.

When I asked her about them, she began to cry. She said her mother forced her to have sex with men, and when she refused, her mother would tie her to the bed with a cord. We were both twelve years old.

If there were too many men in the morning before Zelda went to school, her mother would charge them extra. When I went upstairs to use the bathroom, it was not uncommon to see men sitting in the hallway and down the stairway, waiting their turn with my twelve-year-old friend.

Before long, I began using the bathroom by the kitchen.

I saw men coming and going all day long, and Zelda told me what was going on in those rooms. She said her mother wanted to know if I was interested in becoming one of the working girls. Zelda cried and said she didn't want to ask me, but her mother made her do it. I told her no, and she reported my reply back to her mother, who got angry and sent word back to me as to how much money I could be making.

No amount of money would make me change my mind.

* * *

There were two brothers in the area, Wyatt and Virgil James. For some odd reason, their parents had named them after Wyatt Earp and his brother.

Well, Wyatt liked me, but I was only fourteen and he was twenty-three. His brother was twenty-seven and married. They would get dropped off at the end of the road after working with Daddy at the plant, and I would go down and meet Daddy on the road.

Wyatt would come back to the house with Daddy and just hang around and sit with me on the porch. I wasn't interested in marrying anyone in those hills, let alone a man who was almost ten years older than me.

One night as I was sitting on the porch, he went inside and asked Daddy if he could court me. This made me angry, since I was not interested in him and wished he would just go away. Daddy said he was a nice boy, and I should think about it. I was too young and didn't know what Daddy was thinking!

Wyatt used to wear Brylcreem in his hair, and it always looked greasy and smelled funny. One night, he came down to the holler way after dark. The only light on was the oil lamp in the house, and it put a hazy glow on the dark porch.

I was standing on the porch steps with Wyatt and he said, "I brought you something, a gift." He handed me a small glass bottle. I held it up to the light and could see it had some sort of liquid inside.

"I want you to have it," he said, gushing.

I took it but didn't know what it was nor did I want it. Then he hugged me. I was told that he had been born with a caved-in chest, and I could feel it against mine when he hugged me.

I backed away, repulsed. He tried to kiss me, and I looked away. He thanked me again for accepting his gift, and then he left. I went inside and put the bottle on the mantle. I was just glad he was gone.

The next day, someone saw it and shouted out, "Look what Virgie's got! We saw all the signs! When's it gonna be?"

I had no idea what they were talking about.

It seems the little bottle was filled with urine and a lock of Wyatt's hair, which meant a marriage proposal. By taking the gift from him, I had accepted his hand in marriage!

Wyatt had a sister, Mary Jane, who was in the same grade as me, and she stopped by the house the next day after school.

I told her the mix up, took a piece of poke, and wrote a note for her to give to him. I told him I was sorry, but I had not understood the meaning of his gift, and I hoped he would understand. I told him he was very sweet, but I was not ready at my age to get married. Thank you, but no.

I gave the note and the bottle to Mary Jane, and that night she gave it back to him.

News spread all through the holler that I had refused Wyatt's gift, and I was shunned by everyone in town except for his sister-in-law, Beatrice. Everyone called me stuck up and said I was too good for their mountain boys.

Another time, I was getting ready to go to school when I heard a scream. It was Wyatt's sister-in-law, Beatrice, who lived up the hill behind us. We all ran up there to find her standing on the front porch. She ran into the house, and we followed her inside.

I knew she and Virgil had a baby who was three or four months old, and they'd made a bed for him in the bottom of a dresser drawer. During the night, the baby started crying, so they put him in the bed with them. Sometime during the night, one of them rolled over on top of the baby, smothering him. They woke up and found him dead in the bed next to them.

Virgil built him a tiny coffin that reminded me of the one we put Billy Ray in, and he buried the baby behind their house.

There was boy named Roy Lee whose parents owned the general store alongside the highway. We would stop there for lamp kerosene and groceries. He started coming around to see me, and I guess he was all right.

Nothing exciting, except for the fact that he would bring me a box full of candy from the store. There was gum, Neccos, wax bottles and lips, Mary Janes, Bit-O-Honey. We couldn't afford anything like that, so it was a real treat.

One night when he came up, he said he had to leave town since he'd been drafted into the army and would be sent to Texas. Normally, the boys were sent farther away, so he was glad to still be close. He asked me if I would write to him and wait for him to return. I said no, I wouldn't wait for him, but I would write to him while he was gone.

We wrote back and forth for a while, and then suddenly the letters stopped coming. In the last one, he asked me to come to Texas and live with him. I declined.

A few weeks went by with no word from him, so I figured he had found another girl to be sweet on. I was slightly concerned, since we'd become friends, but I didn't make too much of it until one day when a friend asked me if I'd heard about Roy Lee.

Seems he went AWOL and decided to come home, and he was arrested as soon as he stepped off the train. Ever the romantic, I imagined that I had broken his heart, and he'd left the army to come home to me.

So I did the only thing I could think of and went to the Pikeville jail to visit him. I had never stepped foot inside a jail before, and I was nervous. When I asked to see Roy Lee Mills, the sheriff refused to let me in.

"You Jesse Hopkins's girl, aren't you?" he asked. "He'd be mad as hell you bein' here. You got no business coming in here to see that deserter. You go on home now."

I begged him to let me go back and see him but it was no use so I asked if he would at least let him know that I had been there, he said he would think about it.

I went outside and hollered up to the jail's

second floor windows, hoping Roy Lee might hear me. He saw me and yelled down to me to go home. Said I had no business there, and he didn't want to see me.

The next time I saw him was about a year later. I was getting off the bus into Pikeville, and I had to pass Mills' Country Store. I deliberately crossed the street, because I didn't want to stop.

I saw a man sitting inside the big culvert pipe that ran under the road by the store, but I didn't recognize him. I wasn't going to speak to him, and I hoped he hadn't seen me as I walked past.

He suddenly looked up, saw me and said, "You're pretty."

I thanked him and continued on my way.

He called out, "Wait, don't go. I used to have a girlfriend who looked like you."

"You did?"

He kept his head hung low as he spoke. "She was the prettiest thing I'd ever seen and had these big ol' blue eyes. Do you know her?"

I could see this man had mental problems and wasn't normal, but I said, "I don't know. What was her name?"

"Virgie . . ."

It was Roy Lee! What had happened to him? Had I done this to him? Had the army? The jail? I was not going to engage him in a conversation about anything to do with our past, since we had only been friends and he'd wanted more from me. I edged away slowly. I didn't want him to know I recognized him and wanted to leave.

He kept talking. "You sure are pretty. You

sure you don't know Virgie? What ever happened to her?"

He kept saying it over and over as I walked away. The next thing I heard, he was found dead on the railroad tracks.

Soon I became infatuated with another boy, Chas, who was eighteen. I would dream of him, with his coal-black hair and big, brown eyes. Ever the romantic, I thought maybe we would one day date, marry, and have a beautiful child to match his own beauty.

He moved in down the street and went to work for Cecil Abernathy at his mill. One day when he was returning home, he saw me on the porch, walked over, and sat in the chair next to mine.

He had a younger brother, Andy, who knew I had a crush on his brother and often teased me about it. Chas was unlike the other men who came to the house. He came during the day when Daddy was sometimes home. A lot of men didn't.

As we sat and talked, I imagined being with him, and I listened intently to every word. He was here for the summer, living with his aunt and helping her brother at the mill. It was hard work, he said, but the pay was good, and it gave him spending money and some extra to save for a car.

I had not heard Mom walk up to the screen door until she started screaming at me. "You little slut! Get yourself back in the house!"

I ran into the house with her following after me, calling me vile names.

I wondered what I had done.

A few nights later, I had gotten up during the night to use the bathroom and found Chas and Mom together in her bed. I knew then why she'd been so angry.

When one affair ended, there was always someone else to start another.

Sometimes the plant would shut down, and Daddy would have to go out of town to look for work. I don't know if he would stay away because of work or because of Mom.

She told me years later that Daddy was away because he had a woman friend in Shelby, Kentucky. She said he'd left her without money, and the only way she could buy food was to entertain men. I didn't believe her, though.

Mom began to look at me as her rival. Each affair was a victory she flaunted in triumph. She wanted me to know about her affairs, although she threatened to punish me in many ways if she found out I had allowed a man to touch me.

I was barely a teenager but had the body of a woman. I knew the boys and men looked at my well-developed breasts and made remarks as to their size and how they bounced when I walked.

I was embarrassed that I had no bra to wear or money to buy one, and Mom didn't seem to care. As my breasts increased in size, I tied them down with material I had torn from an old sheet. I hated myself for rubbing lard on them as a kid to make them grow.

Mom need not have feared that I would entice any of her men. I hated every one of them, and I would have killed them if one had tried to touch me.

I became interested in a boy who was close to my own age named Ed Adkins. I was in the eighth grade, and he was a high school quarterback. I only went to the games to see him.

I had a major crush on him, but I was only allowed to date him on Saturday afternoons, which usually meant going to a movie.

One day, some older boys pushed past me and knocked my books out of my hands. Ed saw them do this, picked up my books, and offered to walk me home, which was ten minutes away. I was thrilled that he offered, but embarrassed about living at the Blackburn whorehouse.

Once there, he asked me if he could carry my books for me again the next day, and I said yes. I watched him as he left and was surprised to find that he lived on the other side of the church right next door!

We began going out on Saturdays and spending every moment we could together. I finally told Ed about the whorehouse and about my proposition from Rosie. He was horrified and said he wanted to go there and cuss them out.

Eventually, word leaked out about Rosie's business, and a sheriff showed up at our door with a subpoena to appear in court against her. He told me to give it to my parents, who were not home at the time, so I showed it to Ed first. I did not expect his reaction. He wanted to marry me and take me away from the area, from that life where I feared I would get pregnant at fifteen and have a baby every nine months.

I didn't want to live my life that way, and I thought that by marrying Ed, I might not have to. He would save me from the hell that was my life.

Rosie's trial was a few months away, so I decided to lie about my age, get a license at the courthouse, and get married.

It just so happened that the trial was the same day Ed and I were to meet at the courthouse to get married. At 10:00, I was inside the courtroom to testify against Rosie, and I knew Ed was outside waiting for me. After a while, he left and went home. I was put on the stand, and when Rosie appeared, she lied to the court and said I had been working for her. Mom had to take me to Dr. Day, who had to examine me and offer proof to the court that I was still a virgin and had not been with any man. I was so humiliated and ashamed.

The trial lasted three days, and when I was finally released from my testimony, I went to Ed's to be with him. We decided to postpone our wedding for a while.

After the trial, we moved to Julius Avenue in Pikeville, where we lived in a three-bedroom apartment over a garage owned by Preacher Willis and his family. It was very private. Things were going good.

I was still seeing Ed, Daddy was still at the plant, and Mom seemed to have curved her desire for other men and tried to be a real mother to us. We were able to afford groceries, and we started to feel like a regular family. I was happy.

Daddy and his brother, George, used to go up in the county to Red Creek and Shelby and go fishing on weekends. Suddenly, George stopped going, so Daddy went alone.

One day Uncle George came by and told Daddy, "I can't go fishing with you anymore."

Daddy said, "Well, that's too bad." He didn't know why, but he really didn't care. He enjoyed fishing, whether he had company or not.

Truth was, sixteen-year-old Jenny Tucker was hanging around down by the creek and Uncle George told Daddy, "That kid's gonna get you in trouble."

Well, one day we stopped by to see Uncle Howard and Aunt Elizabeth who lived in Davy, Kentucky, just up the road from Pikeville. Uncle Howard had pigs in the backyard and asked Daddy to come back there and help him. Since I was still his shadow, I followed him while Mom, the little ones, and Aunt Elizabeth were in the house.

From the side of the yard came Jenny. Although she was only sixteen, she was six feet tall and looked like a well-developed twenty-five-year-old woman.

Well, right then and there she said Daddy had gotten her knocked up and wanted to know what he was going to do about it.

Daddy's tan face turned white. He looked at Uncle Howard and then at me, and then he asked where Mom was. I pointed to the house.

He walked inside and Jenny followed him. Daddy was a quiet man, and I never heard any yelling or anything, just the creaking of the front door as it opened. I ran around to see who was leaving. It was Mom.

Daddy didn't say a word, just gathered us up and we left, too.

A few days later, Jewell was acting funny, and I asked her what was wrong. She said Uncle Howard had been putting his hands down her pants. I remembered what he did to me when I was younger, and I was mad as hell.

Not thinking about the consequences, I took Jewell and went back to their house. His mother, Mrs. Ackers was visiting them at the time. I marched up those front steps holding little Jewell's hand and opened their door. They were all sitting in the front room and jumped when I threw the door open.

"Virgie!" Aunt Elizabeth said. "What on earth? Is something wrong?"

"Yes, there's something wrong!" I screamed. "Do you know what my sister told me Uncle Howard has been doing to her?"

So I told them, and I told them about what he had done to me, too.

His mother protested and shouted, "Lies!" and she grabbed me by the arm. "Why would you lie like that about my son?" She grabbed Jewell and pulled her away from me. I snatched her back, and Aunt Elizabeth told me to get out of the house and called me ungrateful.

By that point, Jewell was crying, and Elizabeth had become quiet. I noticed Howard had snuck out the back door. I looked at Aunt Elizabeth. "Say something!"

Mrs. Ackers told us to get out before Howard came back in and they told him what I'd said.

But where were we supposed to go?

We went back home and packed a little suitcase, and Jewell and I decided to leave so Howard wouldn't find us. I had no idea where our parents were.

My Aunt Mabel, Elizabeth's sister, lived nearby. They had married brothers, Howard and Burton. Aunt Mabel lived near the school I had attended when Wade and I were put in foster care with the Hamiltons.

So, I took Jewell and went to Aunt Mabel's where we thought we would be safe. I told her what had happened, and she reached into her fruit jar and gave us the $2.37 she'd saved there. She assured us that we'd done the right thing.

One day, Jewell and I were walking along the railroad tracks. Daddy always said to follow the tracks, and they would lead you into a town. It was still daylight, but I knew it would be dark soon.

As we walked, I heard a noise and turned around. There he was! Uncle Howard was walking down the tracks toward us. I was scared to death, too scared to run.

I whispered to Jewell, "Don't run or look back. Just pretend he's not back there." But I kept looking back to see for myself, and, sure enough, he was still there.

We walked for hours as he snuck along behind us. I remembered how he'd tried to molest me and what he had done to Jewell, and I was terrified of what he might do to us now.

What was he doing back there? He was still following us but just far enough behind to scare us. We were on an isolated mountain railroad track, and it was getting dark. Did anyone, beside Howard, even know or care where we were?

The old tracks snaked their way over a bridge that crossed a river and finally came to a depot. I turned around to see if he was still there, and he was turning around to leave.

We went into the depot and asked how much it would cost for a ticket back into Pikeville. We didn't have enough, so I asked how much it would cost to take us to the nearest town, which was Williamson, West Virginia, thirty-seven miles from Pikeville.

We still didn't have enough; we were short thirteen cents. So I lied and told him Daddy was coming to meet us, and he would pay back the thirteen cents. The clerk refused to sell us a ticket. I was petite for my age and could have passed for someone much younger, so I lied about my age. The clerk still didn't believe me. He insisted that I pay the extra thirteen cents. He motioned me to move along. There were other people behind me, and I was holding up the line.

Jewell and I got out of line and sat on a bench, trying to decide what to do. We were so hungry and tired, and it was getting dark. I was hoping someone would be missing us by now.

A woman walked over to us. I could tell she was a prostitute by the way she wore her clothes and makeup. She took a dollar from her bra and handed it to me. I thanked her but refused. She insisted and forced me to take it from her. I was happy until the clerk told me it would be hours till the next train.

There was a young soldier waiting, too, and he asked us if we were hungry. His mother lived up the holler, and he offered to have her fix us a meal. I said no, but he insisted we'd be safe.

When I refused again, he offered to take us next door to a local restaurant and said he would buy us a meal. But when we got there, they only had a small bowl of apples. I took one, gave Jewell the other one, and told her to hold onto it until later.

The train finally came, and the soldier got on with us. He was nice, and although I didn't say much to him, I appreciated him for trying to help and for not hurting us.

We rode the train into Williamson. When we got off at the station, I lied to the ticket agent and pretended to be looking for Daddy. We were told we had to leave, since the station was closing. I asked if we could stay there, and the ticket agent said no. He told us to go across the street to the Greyhound bus station.

We did, but we knew Daddy wasn't coming; he didn't even know where we were. No one did. I doubt if anyone even cared. We were in a strange town, miles and miles from Pikeville, with no money and no food. When the bus station began to close, I pleaded with the clerk to let us stay. He said we couldn't stay there, but he had a friend who owned a hotel in town, and he would help people who needed a place to stay. I said no.

He took out his wallet, showed us photos of his family and children, and assured us he wouldn't hurt us. It got later and later, and I was scared. Jewell was whining from hunger, so I told her to eat her apple. Reluctantly, I decided to go into town and find the hotel.

Once there, the man showed us the room and gave me a key. Before closing the door, I took one more look around to make sure no one had followed us.

Luckily, there was a phone in the room, and the man told us he would call us when the bus station opened in the morning. I locked the door and put the chain across it, and I pushed the small dresser in front of it. The room was tiny but had a toilet and a sink.

We shared my apple, and although no one bothered us, I was afraid.

The next morning, the phone rang, and we got up and went to the bus station. We were so hungry but had no money for food. I didn't know how we were going to pay for a bus ticket. The ticket back to Pikeville was $2.76. The clerk told me he would give us a free ticket if we promised that our father would send him back the money. Daddy never did.

We finally got back home to Pikeville and went to our apartment on Julius Avenue. We went up the stairs to the door. It was locked. We looked in the windows, and all the furniture was gone, the place was empty. We went next door to Preacher Willis's, but they weren't home. Although he was a minister, he and his wife owned an antique shop downtown.

As we made our way off the steps, Mrs. Breeden from next door called out to me.

"Virgie, your mama and daddy are gone, honey. They moved out last night."

What? They left us? Where did they go?

I knew Daddy's plant was about three miles down the road, so we headed in that direction.

It was hot, and we were tired, thirsty, and hungry. I was always hungry. We were hoping that when we got there, Daddy would give us a bottle of pop.

He was shocked to see us, and he didn't seem too happy. I told him what had happened but not about Uncle Howard. No one believed me anyway, so why tell?

Daddy didn't seem too concerned about us being gone and, as was his quiet way, said nothing.

I was hoping for a hug, at the very least, but there was none.

Red Creek, Kentucky

Mom left Daddy, and I was surprised. She cheated on Daddy so many times and even gave birth to another man's child, and he overlooked each and every time. He did the same thing to her and she leaves?

Daddy got himself a little trailer so he could be near Jenny and had taken Wade with him. We waited for Daddy to get off work, and he took me and Jewell to stay with him and Wade.

Daddy said he had to wait for thirty days for his divorce from Mom to be final so he could marry Jenny. He didn't want to divorce her, but Jenny's family was forcing him to do it and marry their pregnant daughter.

No matter what Mom put him through, he loved her, and I knew he would till the day he died. I hated Jenny, her family, and the whole nasty situation.

The trailer was a dump and smelled like garbage. Jenny and her family were pure mountain hillbillies.

The trailer was barely big enough for Daddy and Wade, but Jenny was there, too, with her whole family: her mother, Nadine; sisters Mary, Ethyl, Zelva, and Helen; and brothers Dewey Ray, Timmy, and Percy. Zelva was nine, the same age as Jewell. Brother Percy was twelve, like Wade, and Bobbie Jo and I were both fourteen.

Her father, Adolph—"Dolph," for short—was living there, too. He had been injured in The

Great War and had been poisoned by mustard gas. He stayed in the back bedroom and was emaciated and covered in bedsores. They kept a light sheet on him, and, to my knowledge, he was only fed once in a while.

He would moan and call out crazy talk at all hours of the day and night, and I thought each and every time he was dying. He smelled like urine and feces, and I couldn't say which smelled worse, him or the trailer.

The whole hillbilly clan—plus Daddy, me, Wade, and Jewell—all lived in one tiny trailer.

On top of everything else, we were forced to share each other's clothing. They smelled horrible, and I was embarrassed to wear them. At least Mom had kept us clean, and our home and clothes always smelled fresh. I hated sharing my clothes with such disgusting people, so I used to hide mine so no one could find them and want to wear them.

Where was Mom?

Eventually, we all moved to Red Creek, which was eleven miles outside of Pikeville. We moved into a little wooden house for veterans, given to Dolph for his services in the war.

It came with a small piece of land and had four rooms but no heat or electricity. There were two fireplaces and a cookstove. I never got a chance to see Ed and tell him we were moving. I cared about him and missed him. I hoped he knew I still wanted to be with him.

I found out later that Mom had gone to stay with Uncle Howard and Aunt Elizabeth. Howard's friend, Albert Ainsworth, had come home on leave from the army, where he was stationed in Texas. He offered to take Mom back with him and she went.

* * *

It was 1943, and I was fourteen years old. I went to school every day in a one-room schoolhouse that was about a two-mile walk from our house. All six grades were in one room; each row was another grade.

We had no money to buy lunch, but through a government program, lunch was furnished to the students. Every day we got a two-ounce can of pork and beans, crackers, a wooden spoon, and a small carton of milk. I hated school, but I went so I could eat.

The bathroom for our house was across the creek. The little shack of an outhouse leaned over the creek, and when you went to the bathroom, it all just dropped down into the water below.

The house was always filthy, and everyone in the family had to share the one towel we owned.

In order to wash clothes, Jenny had to build a fire out back and sit a large tub on the flames, fill it with water from the creek, throw the clothes in, and stir them with a stick. No wonder they smelled bad!

It was a miserable place to live, and I hated being there. I always felt like I was in the way.

There was no place to sleep; there were only two beds in the house, and they were for the adults. I had to bundle up the clothes I found scattered around the house, put them on the floor by the fireplace, and use that as my bed. I had to share the bedclothes and the floor with the other children.

I was always hungry, and I looked forward to summertime so I could sneak into other people's gardens and steal vegetables. I would take a poke and fill it with all the wild greens I could carry.

By now, Daddy and Jenny were married. She did little cooking, and we didn't get along well at all. At fourteen, I didn't enjoy having a sixteen-year-old stepmother.

Her sister, Helen, would make a breakfast of gravy, biscuits, and fatback. She would leave it on the stove, and whoever got up first got to eat. The men were always up first since they worked. If you were lazy or too tired to get up, you didn't eat. Needless to say, the adults were always up before us, so we went to school hungry every day.

Not once did anyone in that house offer to feed us kids. We were on our own.

* * *

There were a lot of strange people living in the area.

One was a boy named Sam, though we knew him as "Fuzzy." He was retarded, and he would come over to see us every day and just hang out. His sister, Tootie, would come along, too. We never made fun of him, but we used to call him Fuzzy Wuzzy.

This big ol' boy was about fourteen and didn't have a lick of sense. He didn't go to school and didn't seem to have a real home to go to. I felt sorry for him. It was common back then for people to hang out at other people's houses. There was nothing to do in those hills, so people liked to socialize to pass the time.

One time, a few days went by, and they didn't come by. Then out of the blue, his sister came by alone, and we asked about Fuzzy.

"Well," she said, "he done got smart with Daddy the other night, and Daddy wasn't having none of it. He took a piece of stove wood and hit Fuzzy in the head with it. He fell down on the floor, and when Daddy went to get him up, he wouldn't move. So he left him lie there all day, and Mother went to check on him once in a while. He lay there all day long, and finally Daddy dug a hole and put Fuzzy in it."

Another time, we heard about a woman who lived a few miles down the road from us. She lived way out in the country, back on a long, dirt road. Seems she was pregnant and was craving canned peaches.

The weather had turned ugly, and a terrible snowstorm had come in and blocked the road to their house. She was in an awful way and pleaded with her husband to get some peaches for her and their unborn baby. So he put on a pair of boots and trudged through the snowstorm.

He finally made it to the main road, but the town was still miles away. His love for his wife and baby were so strong, he walked the many miles into town, found the store, and bought her all the canned peaches he could carry.

While he was in the store, the snow picked

up, and he was advised by the shop owner to stay put until the storm passed. Against his better wishes, he did so, and he was unable to get back home until the next morning.

When he got back inside, his pregnant wife lay on the bed, dead. Distraught with grief and overcome with guilt, he opened the peaches and began feeding her with a spoon.

Days later when the snow had stopped, some neighbors went back to check on them and found that he had gone insane and was still feeding peaches to his dead wife.

Another story Daddy would tell us was hard to believe, but it made a good story on cold, spooky nights. There was an old woman named Anna Mae Goodwin who lived in a cottage on the edge of town. She wasn't a friendly woman, nor was she liked by many of the townspeople. She would come into town every day at the same time and go to the store to buy sugar, salt, and molasses.

She was called many names by people, but the one that caught my attention was witch. The story was that Anna Mae had the magic ability to turn herself into any animal she wanted. She could be a cat, a crow, a horse . . . anything.

Well, according to Daddy, a neighbor of hers, Mr. Johnston, heard a noise in his backyard one night. Looking out, he saw a black cow eating his garden. He ran outside and yelled for it to get on home, and it did.

The next night, the same thing happened. This went on for about a week. Finally he'd had enough. On the last night, he waited for the cow to come into the garden, and when it did, he threw an ax at it and hit it in the hind leg. It did not return.

Several days went by, and Anna Mae had not come into town to do her regular shopping. After a week, some of the menfolk decided they should check on her. Walking into her house, they found rotting vegetables on the kitchen table and floor and Anna Mae in her bedroom, dead. One of her legs had been cut off, and Mr. Johnston's ax was on the floor by her bed.

There was another man in town known as Earl. He had been discharged from the service and sent back home to Kentucky. He looked so handsome in his uniform, and when he walked by the house, I would watch him as everyone hollered at him from their porch and gave him a hero's welcome.

I didn't know much about him except his name, but I began asking around. It seems his wife cheated on him and left him brokenhearted, so he ran off and joined the service. He'd been sent home on a Section Eight discharge.

Back then, we had no regular mail delivery. A mail truck delivered mail on the highway, but down in the holler you never knew when the mail was coming, if ever.

We didn't have a mailbox, and if mail came to us at all, it went to Adkins Country Store, General Delivery. Every time I saw Earl go by to wait for the mail, I went down to wait with him. I would sit on a rock and wait for the truck. I never got any mail, though; I just liked spending time with him.

We would sit and talk, and he'd cry about his wife and the things he'd seen and done in the service. I would listen to him for hours. I was such a romantic! I thought for sure I could mend his broken heart and make it all better for him.

One day he passed the house, and he was stumbling and wondered off down by the creek. I watched as he fell facedown in the water. I went to save him. I turned his face out of the water, which was just a little trickle and not much of a creek at the time.

Daddy came home and saw us and ran down to the creek. When he saw Earl drunk and sprawled in the water, he grabbed me by the arm and said, "Don't you ever talk to this drunk again!" Then he told me to go up on the porch, and he sent Earl home.

When Daddy came in, he gave me hell and told me Earl was nothing but a drunk, and he was "sick in the head." I was told to have nothing to do with the man.

He still passed the house on occasion, and he was either drunk or on his way to being there.

* * *

Not everyone in the house was mean to me. I liked Jenny's sister, Helen, who was always nice. Well, Helen got married and built a house next door to us. She was already pregnant when they said their vows, and when the time came to give birth, her husband called on the birthing woman who lived down the street.

I was there when baby Larry was born at our house. The birthing woman cut the cord too short, and blood squirted out everywhere. She ran to the fireplace, grabbed a handful of soot, and put it on the open wound.

The bleeding stopped immediately.

By now, there was another terrible war going on across the ocean. War plants were opening up in Detroit, Michigan, and it seemed everyone was headed up north. Helen went there and sent word back that the wages were good and encouraged everyone to follow her.

Women were joining the workforce to replace men who had gone off to war, and President Roosevelt was encouraging everyone's support for our efforts back home.

Nestled in the hills of Appalachia, however, the war seemed a million miles away to me. Daddy didn't want us to move to Detroit. He was a southern boy and said we were staying in Kentucky. Besides, Jenny was due to have their baby any day, and he didn't want to leave her side.

I still didn't like Jenny. Not only was the closeness in age a problem, but before she met Daddy she had a boyfriend named Dodge. Unknown to Daddy, she was still seeing him on the side while Daddy was at work.

Aside from sleeping with her ex-boyfriend, she did nothing all day but lie on the couch. She was one of the dirtiest and laziest people I'd ever met.

She and Daddy didn't get along. Not once did I see the love and closeness I saw with him and Mom. I never saw her bake a white cake or bleach the floor. I never saw him smack her on the backside and call her honey girl, like he did Mom.

I hated that he and Mom were apart, but I hated her more for leaving us.

The winters were harsh and I struggled to survive. The house was always cold, and Jewell and I didn't have a coat or a sweater to wear. I pestered Daddy to buy us one, but he never did. No one cared about us; were just objects, things.

After a while, I guess he got tired of me bugging him, because he promised to go out that weekend and get me and Jewell a coat.

When the weekend arrived and Daddy went into town, I was so excited and looked forward to my new coat. But when he came home, he'd bought Jenny one instead. It was a long, wool coat with red, green, and yellow plaid designs. She came in wearing it, showing it off to the rest of us. Daddy stayed outside and didn't come in.

I was mad for me, but sad for Jewell. We were both so cold.

Right then and there, I thought of Daddy as a coward. I'd never thought that way of him before. I used to worship him, but now I had no respect for him. Since getting involved with Jenny and her family, he was a different man.

I resented Jenny and her new coat. The more I stewed, the madder I got. Daddy kept telling me to calm down and not upset the other children, but I didn't care. He no longer cared about me or his other kids with Mom. He had a new family now with Jenny and her hillbillies, and he was about to be a father again any day.

The living conditions were so horrible and tense that Jenny and I got into a fight every day. Lately, however, the fights were about the coat. One fight was particularly vicious.

It was cold, and there was a fire burning in the fireplace. I picked up a piece of wood from the stack on the hearth and yelled at her, “I will take this piece of wood and hit you in the belly and get rid of that little bastard you’re carrying!”

Her brother, Dewey Ray, was in the kitchen. He came out and stood in the doorway carrying something in his hand. He threw it at me, and it hit me in the head and knocked me out cold. It was a can of condensed milk.

Dewey Ray was a pig. He was sixteen and a big ol’ mountain boy. He smelled like lard and always had a trail of tobacco juice running down his chin. I think he was retarded, but he had the strength of two grown men.

After that fight, he tried to kill me several times, and if he wasn’t trying to do me in, he was trying to get in my pants. I would run and hide in the corner behind the couch, but he would find me, grab me, throw me down, and slobber all over me. I was always fighting him off.

Once when I was running from him, he got mad because I was resisting him. He grabbed me and threw me on the ground. I thought for sure he was going to rape me right there in front of everyone. I kicked him and was able to get up and run into the house. I must have hurt his manhood, because he ran into the house after me and got his shotgun. I ran to my usual place behind the couch, and he came in and saw me.

"You get your skinny ass outta there and give me some, or I'm gonna shoot you," he called out.

I stood up. The gun was pointed right at my chest. I started crying and begged him not to shoot me. Suddenly, I decided to jump back down on the floor behind the couch, and the gun went off. It put a huge, gaping hole in the wall above me.

That was it. I decided to leave right then and there. I could no longer live in that horrible place with those horrible people Daddy now called family. They were not *my* family, and he obviously wasn't anymore, either.

He and Jenny's baby was born that winter. It was 1944, and I was fifteen years old.

Not long after the gun incident, my Aunt Ruby and Uncle Charlie came for a visit. While they were there, I asked if I could go live with them. My aunt was one of Daddy's sisters and a very softhearted woman. They lived in Tennessee, and I thought that was far enough from Kentucky for me. I was thrilled when they agreed to take me back with them.

* * *

Uncle Charlie got a job in Cumberland Gap, which is located just north of the spot where Kentucky, Tennessee, and Virginia meet. He managed a gas station there, and the three of us lived in the small apartment over the garage.

One night, I heard a noise downstairs in the garage. I got up and could hear Uncle Charlie yelling and cussing. I thought maybe it was robbers come to rob the gas station.

I ran to the windows but couldn't see the gas pumps because of the roof over them. Then Aunt Ruby got up to see what was going on.

Suddenly, I heard Ed's voice outside.

"Get your goddamned ass back to Pikeville! She's not going anywhere with you!" Uncle Charlie yelled.

I heard Ed tell my uncle that he had no idea where I'd moved, but he'd finally found me and to please let him see me. He had come all the way down from Pikeville to get me. My uncle saw me at the window and told me to stay put.

In the dim light, I saw Ed pleading with my uncle to see me. I banged on the window, but he didn't hear me. He got in his truck and drove off. I cried and cried all night.

I got a job at a local hardware store. My uncle dropped me off at work every day. I got paid fifteen dollars each week, in one-dollar bills.

My plan was to save my money and then go back to Pikeville to find Ed. I lied to my aunt and uncle about how much money I made, although I did give a little to Aunt Ruby every week to help out. I hid the rest.

One day on my way home from work, I walked to the post office and mailed a letter to Ed. I told him I was saving up enough money to come see him in Kentucky.

It took a few months for me to save enough money to get back to Pikeville. When I had enough, my uncle dropped me off at work, and I pretended to go inside. As soon as his car was out of sight, I walked to the bus station and bought a ticket.

Once back in Pikeville, I searched for Ed. It had been a while since the night he came to Tennessee to get me, but I was glad I'd been able to send him a letter that I was coming back to be with him. When I got to his house, his mother and sister were there and were surprised to see me.

"Why, Virgie Hopkins! What on earth are you doing back here? We thought you moved to Tennessee."

I explained to them that I had moved and about Ed coming to get me, about the letter, and about everything! I was so excited to be in his house again, to be able see him again, that I nearly stuttered all my words.

They looked at each other, and his mother lowered her eyes. "Honey, Ed never got no letter from you. Are you sure you mailed it to the right address?"

"Yes!" I said. I was sure. I could tell something was wrong.

"Where is he, Mrs. Adkins? I have to see him!"

"Virgie, when Ed came back from Tennessee, he was a broken man. He loved you and went there to get you, to marry you, but your uncle told him to go away. He said you didn't want anything to do with Ed. I can see now that was not the case."

"Where is he?" I cried.

"He up and joined the navy just a few days after coming back home. I'm sorry, Virgie."

I was heartbroken and didn't know what to do. However, I wanted to see Daddy while I was in town, so I went to the Pepsi-Cola plant.

I had no money to get back to Tennessee, so I went back to live with him and Jenny. I had nowhere else to go.

I hated to go back to Red Creek, but several months had gone by, and I'd hoped the living conditions might have improved. If anything, they'd gotten worse. Jenny was pregnant again, and I wondered if the baby belonged to Daddy or to Dodge.

I stayed with Daddy for a while but wanted to see Mom. She'd come to Tennessee and discovered I was gone, so she'd taken Jewell back with her to Pikeville. Daddy said Mom got a job as a hired girl for the Miller family. I hadn't seen her in a few months, so I walked the eleven miles to the bridge that took me into Pikeville.

It was fifteen miles to the Miller's.

Once there, I asked her if I could stay with her. I told her about the living conditions with Daddy, but she said I couldn't stay. They only allowed one child to be there with her.

The Millers had a huge house that looked like a mansion to me. They were kind enough to allow Mom to let Jewell stay there with them in an upstairs bedroom.

I always wondered if I would be living there

with her instead of Jewell, had I been there the day Mom came back. I would have loved to live in a nice, big, clean home instead of a tiny trashy one full of crazy hillbillies.

I cried to Mom to let me stay with her, but she insisted I go back to Red Creek. I didn't want to, but I had nowhere else to go.

Finally, Mom relented and said I could stay with her until she found somewhere better for us to live. She said I'd have to hide and not let the Millers know I was living there.

So, I moved in with Mom and Jewell, and Mom would sneak food upstairs to me. Once she brought me up a whole box of Ritz crackers. I was not allowed to go downstairs, although the Millers were gone most of the day. Mom knew she had to find another place for me to live.

There was an old woman in town named Mrs. Ainsworth. Her son, Albert, was in the army and was the same man Mom had run off with when Daddy got Jenny pregnant.

Mrs. Ainsworth said she was crippled, although the doctor said there was nothing wrong with her. The old woman needed someone to help care for her, and Mom told me to stay with her and help her.

She was a nasty old bitch who had me run errands for her all day long and treated me like dirt. Mrs. Ainsworth was insane, but it seems she wasn't always that way. She kept a shoebox on the nightstand next to the bed. In it were a set of false teeth belonging to her sweetheart, Joe, who had died many years before. At night, I could hear her talking to those filthy teeth.

She refused to walk or get out of bed, and I had to do everything for her. I told her the doctor said she should try to walk, but she just cussed me and told me she wasn't paying me to offer her medical advice.

I left her when her fifteen-year-old granddaughter came into town to help her instead. Later on, we found out the young girl had committed suicide while living there.

Not long after, Mrs. Ainsworth's house caught fire, but since she was "crippled," she couldn't get out of bed. Actually, she had confined herself to her bed for so long, her legs were useless, and she could no longer walk. She burned to death in her bed.

After the fire, they found her body at the bottom of the hill. It had been decapitated. The head was still in her bed.

I got another housekeeping job and moved in with the family I was working for, a young couple with two children. The woman was pregnant again, and the husband was a manager of Walgreens drug store. I was just glad to have a place to live and food to eat.

One day, the wife sent me to the store to buy lamb chops. Well, I had never seen a lamb chop in my life but was too embarrassed to tell them and bought the wrong kind of meat by mistake.

When I got back, she yelled at me and called me stupid. After they all went to bed, I left them. I felt bad, though, because the next day, she had her baby and didn't have any help.

By now, I'd found it too hard to continue going to school while trying to survive and find enough to eat, so I quit in the eighth grade.

Besides, I was constantly being teased and called the daughter of the town whore. I got tired of all the boys picking on me and the girls snickering behind my back. I had no friends, except the two young whores from the whorehouse, which didn't make it any easier on me at school.

My next housekeeping job was for another couple, the Goodmans, who had two smart-ass daughters I despised. They had been in my class before I quit school, and they were mean to me because I was now working for their parents.

The family owned a car dealership and had money, so the daughters always had nice things and pretty clothes to wear. The mother used to pack up the dresses the girls had outgrown and put them in storage.

Well, I had never stolen anything in my life—except vegetables when I was hungry—but I wanted one of those dresses for Jewell. They were so pretty and dainty. The girls had no use for them, and I didn't see the harm in taking one or two . . . or three. I gave the three little dresses to Mom to give to Jewell, and they fit her perfectly.

At the house, I did all the cooking, cleaning, and ironing. One day after I'd done all the chores downstairs, I went upstairs to make the bed.

On the bedroom dresser was the most beautiful ring I had ever seen. It had a red, sparkly center that looked like a large, red diamond. I admired it so much that I put it on my ring finger and started to make the bed. I forgot I was wearing it until the woman came home and saw it on my finger. I was not going to steal it. I was just admiring it and forgot to take it off.

She grabbed my hand and twisted my finger to remove it. I was frightened.

"You stole my ring!" she screamed.

I lied to her and told her my boyfriend had given it to me. Finally, I took it off and handed it back to her.

I admitted that I had lied, but I explained that I wasn't going to steal it. I only wanted to wear it for a little while to feel pretty. She lectured me about lying and stealing, so I left that night after they all went to bed.

I was always running away without telling people. I never had anyone to turn to. I was only fifteen years old and was basically alone in the world.

I ended up taking a cleaning job for a woman named Annie Newton, who owned a photo shop. As the hired girl, it was my job to clean the shop and keep the place organized. In return, I was allowed to live in the back room of the shop.

Annie was a stylish, artsy kind of woman who liked to eat fresh chicken. Part of my job was to go out back, catch a chicken, lay its head on a block, and cut it off.

Unknown to me, Mrs. Goodman had told Annie about the ring incident. One early morning, Annie's yelling woke me from a sound sleep. "I knew I shouldn't have trusted you!"

She accused me of stealing her bracelet—I had not—and she threatened to call the police if I didn't return it. I begged and pleaded with her not to call the police. I didn't have her bracelet, but she didn't believe me and threw me out of the shop.

Once again, I was out on the street.

Some of the girls in town tried to get me to become a prostitute, telling me how much money I could be making.

They said I was sure pretty enough to be making twenty dollars a day, which was a lot of money to me at that time. They told me they were charging between one and five dollars a turn for each man, and they could easily make more money in one day than I was making in several as a hired girl.

I was homeless, starving, lonely, and scared, and I must admit I was tempted, but I chose not to go down that path.

My next job was for another young couple, the Dodsons, who had a three-year-old daughter named Hattie. She couldn't speak, so I tried to teach her to say a few words. Mrs. Dodson was nice, and she trusted me to babysit for her. She also showed me how to set a table and how to wash dishes properly. I slept in a screened-in room on the back porch.

One day, Mrs. Dodson told me how grateful she was for my help with Hattie, and she wanted to reward me with a permanent for my hair. I had long, blonde hair, and I had never been to a beauty shop before and was very excited.

The girl began shampooing my hair, and it felt nice to have the warm suds on my head. Suddenly she stopped, and I could hear her whispering to the other woman.

She was nice but whispered to me that my long hair was full of head lice.

They put in a tonic called Larkspur that smelled horrible and turned my hair a light shade of red. They put a towel on my head and told me to sit there while the tonic was working.

I was so humiliated and embarrassed, I wanted to die.

The two women kept looking at each other, and they told me I couldn't get a permanent there. My long hair would have to be cut short instead.

After I left the beauty shop, I ran away. I couldn't face Mrs. Dodson. She had been so nice to me. I was so embarrassed!

I did just what you'd expect: I ran.

Nurses Training

As the war escalated, there was a huge government plea for trained nurses and hospital personnel.

The hospital in Pikeville was a spooky old place that sat on the hill overlooking the town. It reminded me of a haunted castle. I went up there and talked to Dr. Ashley, the administrator. They offered me a nursing course, and I could live in the dorm across the street while I attended school.

The only problem was I had to be eighteen to take the course, and I was only sixteen. When I told them I was homeless and needed a job, they let me enroll anyway. I made thirty dollars a month and got a nurse's uniform; plus, I got to eat all the free food I wanted at the hospital cafeteria.

I was in heaven!

It was the ideal place for me, and I enjoyed it there. I loved the training, the medical knowledge, the feel and sound of the starched, white uniform. Most of all, I loved helping others and seeing the smile of a patient as I entered the room.

I soon earned the nickname "Sunshine," since they said when I entered a room, it filled with sunshine.

I was so proud when I earned my first cap, but there was no one from my family to see me at the presentation. But their absence didn't shadow my happiness.

Since there was a shortage of nurses, I was thrown into actual hospital experience and assigned duties that, in peace time, would only have been assigned to fully-trained nurses.

Each day, I was responsible for the complete care of as many as twenty patients. This care would encompass everything from the emptying of bed pans to the giving of injections and the taking of blood samples for the lab.

On our lunch break, the other students and I would practice giving injections by using an orange to simulate an arm or testing the hypodermic needles by pulling them through a ball of cotton. If the tip of the needle was too dull to obtain the cotton, it was discarded. I hated to throw them away, because it was difficult to acquire hypodermic needles and syringes at that time, as they were needed on the battlefields.

We used and rationed all our medical supplies for as long as possible.

We were told in training not to become emotionally attached to our patients. Mrs. Hill, our instructor, told us, "Always be detached. Do not, I repeat, do not involve yourself with your patients. Do your duty in a kindly and orderly manner. An emotional nurse is not a good or useful nurse."

Although I believed that, it was hard for me not to care about them on a personal level.

But I learned my lesson with a young patient named Allan Spaulding, who was just a few years older than me.

He was dying from colon cancer, and most of the time he was sedated. However, there were times when he was fully awake and rational and asked that I read or talk to him. We became friends as the weeks passed, and it broke my heart to see him linger in the in-between world of the living and the dead.

I found myself going to the library to find books he might enjoy. On the way to the hospital, I picked wild flowers to brighten his room. I even took him my radio so he could listen to music.

I went against all my teachings, and I could hear Mrs. Hill scolding me in the back of my mind. But I would do anything to make his last days on earth happy ones.

One morning, I awoke with the feeling that something was wrong. The old familiar ESP was kicking in, and I remember Daddy telling me that although it was a gift, at times I would think it a curse. I quickly showered and dressed, and as I walked outside, I shivered. In Kentucky, we were fortunate to have long summers and cool evenings but it still got cold in the winter. It was the last week of November, and until today, the temperature had been in the sixties.

I ran across the street to the hospital, and before removing my coat, I reached for the patient chart that read *Allan Spaulding, age 24, Protestant, Dr. Hilliary.* I checked the note from the night nurse. The patient had asked not to be given anything to help him sleep. I thought maybe I'd been wrong about my "feeling."

I filled the water pitchers, placed them on the cart, and began my rounds. I stopped at the linen closet to pick up fresh linens, and I remembered that in my haste I had forgotten the thermometers which were to be given to my patients before the ice water.

As I entered the diet kitchen, I heard one of the student nurses talking to someone on the phone. I stopped when I heard the name Allan Spaulding.

She said, "Yes, ma'am. I'm off duty right now, but I'll tell Miss Hopkins, his day nurse. Oh yes, he seems so much better this morning. In fact, he asked me not to give him a sleeping pill last night. He said he wanted to be bright and alert today. Maybe he knew you were coming and wanted to be fully awake so as to enjoy your visit. Yes, at 1:00. I won't forget. You're welcome. Good-bye."

I waited as she hung up the phone.

"Oh Virgie, I didn't know you were there, or I would have given you the phone. That was Allan Spaulding's mother. She lives in Chicago, and she just heard from a relative about him being in the hospital. She's coming on the 1:00 train to see him. Will you be sure and tell him? I understand they haven't seen each other in ten years."

I said I would, but I wondered why he'd had no visitors before now.

She went on to explain that his mother said she and Allen's father divorced when he was fourteen. Allen chose to live with his father, but no one seemed to know his whereabouts. Poor Allen, I felt even closer to him now.

It was almost 10:30 before I finished the other rooms. I always saved his for last so we would have more time together. As I reached his room, the door was ajar, so I knocked lightly and entered. I stepped back into the hall when I saw one of the male aides changing the tube that led from his penis to the urine bottle hanging on the side of the bed.

As I waited, I returned the pitchers and thermometers to the diet kitchen and placed the used linens down the laundry chute. When I returned to Allan's room, the aide was gone.

I was so happy to see him, and I knew he felt the same way. We laughed and talked as I changed his linens, and I gave him the message from his mother. He commented on his apprehension at seeing her again after so many years, and he asked me to get his doctor's permission to go outside.

He said he wanted to see the fall leaves for the last time.

I turned and choked back tears at his remark. I knew I should never have become so close to this dying man. I promised him I would ask.

I stayed as long as I possibly could and then reminded him that I would see him in less than an hour with his lunch tray.

Lunch time came and, once again, I saved his tray for last. I was humming as usual when I opened his door, and I could smell the aroma of fried chicken, his favorite, coming from under the covered dish.

I placed the tray on the bedside table and chatted with him as I reached down to roll up the head of his bed so he could eat. He did not reply when I told him I'd gotten permission from his doctor to take him outside.

As I raised the bed rails, I looked up to find sightless, brown eyes staring back at me.

I jumped back. The glow was gone from his eyes, and I knew at that second he was gone. As if in a trance, I pressed the call button to summon another nurse.

Short staffed, the head nurse, Mrs. Summers came into the room, complaining about how she couldn't finish her lunch without interruption. I hadn't moved. I couldn't force my eyes away from his. I could hear Mrs. Summers yelling at me, as if in a dream.

"Miss Hopkins, place your fingers on his eyelids, and hold them there for a few moments until they stay closed. Remove the tube from his penis, and take the urine bottle out of the room before it gets knocked over. The stink would be terrible!"

She looked up as I made no effort to follow her instructions. I couldn't force myself to touch him. She screamed at me to leave the room and to get someone in there who knew what they were doing.

The sound of her voice was enough to summon several nurses who ran into the room. She screamed at one of them to take me to her office, and I was to stay there until she arrived.

I waited in stunned silence for what I knew would be a severe reprimand. I didn't have long to wait. She came into the room, slamming the door behind her, and stood over me a full minute before she spoke.

"Would you be kind enough to tell me what happened to you in there? What kind of nurse are you going to make if you can't carry out a simple order like closing the eyes of a deceased patient? If you do continue your training and graduate, you'll see many patients die, and you'll be asked to do a lot more than close their eyes. Now you go out there, get Mr. Spaulding's chart, and record the time of his death, as close as possible. I have called for two wards to place the body on the cart. You will take him downstairs to the morgue, fill out the necessary papers, and return to duty. You have other patients to care for."

I wanted to tell her that Allan had been different. That he was more than a patient to me; he was my friend.

I wanted to tell her that for a short time, I had dreamed he would someday recover from his illness, and we would date, go to the movies, take long walks along the river, and perhaps, someday, we would fall in love, marry, and live a long and happy life together.

I knew she wouldn't understand.

I also knew Mrs. Summers was right in reprimanding me. I'd been taught to do as I'd been told. I had failed in my duties, and she had every right to report me to her supervisor, as I was certain she would.

She was reaching the age of retirement, and she didn't want to antagonize the front office by not following the rules. Our current administrator, Dr. Jonas, was young, energetic, and eager, and he believed in early retirement and young replacements.

As I was leaving her office, one of the wards

called out to me. “Virgie, Mr. Spaulding is ready when you are. I called downstairs to tell them you were bringing him down.”

I mumbled a thank you as I walked over to the green-sheet-covered body that lay on the cart. I tried to pretend that it was someone I didn’t know.

I tried to concentrate on the numbers above the elevator as I waited for it to reach my floor, but my eyes kept falling back to the cart. I traced the outline of his body beneath the sheet, and I ached for all my unspoken dreams.

The Bucket of Blood

While I was in nurses training, Mom lost her job with the Millers. She was able to find a room in a boardinghouse known as the "Bucket of Blood." Jewell had gone back to live with Daddy and Jenny, so I agreed to move back in with her. She didn't want to be alone.

The Bucket of Blood had been a tavern before it was turned into a rooming house. The old house had porches on both sides and was owned by Dean and Eliza Profitt.

Mom had a small, two-room apartment upstairs. The room next to hers was occupied by Dean's brother, Ralph, and on the other side of his room was mine.

Although I was living with Mom again, I was still attending nursing school. Instead of living in the dorm across the street from the hospital, I now had to walk eleven miles each way, every morning and every night, to attend school.

For some odd reason, I never had any fear of walking home alone after dark. I guess after all I'd been through, walking alone at night was no big deal.

Mom kept telling me about this cute young man and his grandmother, who had a herd of cows in the field across from the rooming house.

Her name was Mary Margaret Magdalene, and she was married to a man with the last name McCoy. She was renting out the field to house the cows, and the boy came up every afternoon and tended to the cattle.

His name was Billy Justice. I would sit on the front porch and watch him, but he couldn't see me. He never wore a shirt, and his tan, muscular body glistened with sweat in the summer sun. His hair was black as coal dust, and he had big, dark eyes to match. I swear he had to be the prettiest boy I'd ever seen.

Mom knew him and his grandmother, so I begged her to introduce me to him. One day when he was finishing up with the cattle, we walked over there. He was painfully shy and didn't say much, so Mom invited him over to visit us sometime.

I was worried at first. He looked a lot like Daddy as a young man, and I remembered what happened the last time I liked a boy but didn't know he was involved with my own mother.

But this time it seemed okay.

Well, every day after tending to the cattle, he would come by for a glass of sweet tea, and we would sit on the porch and talk. This went on for about six months, but he was too shy to ask me out on a date.

We were both sixteen, though he might have been closer to seventeen. He said his family lived in Virginia, and they raised horses. He was only visiting his grandmother and helping her out with the cows.

I was still working at the hospital, and one night I ran into a girl I knew. She asked me if I knew Billy Justice. I said, "Yes, isn't he the cutest thing?"

She said, "Why yes, he is! I can't wait til Saturday night when we go out on a date."

She said she "sorta" asked him out, and he "sorta" said yes. I was so jealous.

The next time I saw him go past the house, I walked over to the field to see him. I was wearing a white peasant blouse that I pulled down over my shoulders and a pair of shorts. I flirted openly with him.

That night, we went to the carnival together. While there, we ran into the girl from the hospital, and she was madder than a wet hen. She never spoke to me again.

Billy was so nice to me that evening. We rode all the rides and ate cotton candy, and since he didn't have a car, he walked me the five miles back to our house. He was a perfect gentleman, but it frustrated me that he didn't even try to steal a kiss!

Billy knew a lot about the Bucket of Blood. His grandmother told him that when the family took it over, they had the well cleaned out and there were infant skeletons found down there.

The house had been a whorehouse, and when the whores got pregnant, the unwanted babies were disposed of in the well.

I was scared to death to live there after that, and the stories continued.

When I went home, I asked Mrs. Profitt why my room—the walls, the floor, everything—was painted a deep red. There were also tops from tin cans nailed in weird places all over the walls, and they were painted red as well. She shrugged and said it was like that when they moved in. She knew something but didn't want to tell me. I guess if she told her tenants the gory history of the house, no one would want to live there.

One day while I was waiting in the basement for the dryer to finish, Mrs. Owens, who owned a dress shop next door, came in to get a coke from one of the many machines that lined the walls of the basement. She started to leave and had one hand on the door, and then she saw me.

"Hey, aren't you that Hopkins girl who lives in the red room upstairs?"

I nodded that I was.

"Boy," she said, "you sure are brave. You couldn't pay me to spend a night in that room. Everybody knows it's haunted, and it's no wonder, all the things that's gone on in that house."

She pulled up a chair to be closer to me as she talked. "You would not believe the stories that Sarah—she's the girl who helps me at the store—tells me about that house. Do you know it used to be a house of prostitution? Sarah used to clean up the rooms for Mrs. Weddington, who owned it before the Profitts bought it. They found something awful in that well, too. The people and things she saw over there would make your hair stand on end."

My hair was already standing on end, but I didn't want her to see my fear.

She stopped long enough to see if I was shocked. "Have you ever seen or heard anything in that room? It wouldn't surprise me if you did."

I started to tell her that I really didn't want to hear any stories about my room. I had just gotten used to staying by myself after Billy's horror stories, and I didn't want to hear anything that might bring back my fear. However, she had a captive audience as my clothes dried, and she took full advantage of it.

"It was eight or ten years ago," she continued. "I'm not sure of the exact date . . ."

I assured her that it really didn't matter.

"Well," she droned on, "have you met Harold Robins who owns the Robins Nest Café?"

I shook my head.

"Well, the story goes, one day he went home early from the restaurant. Everyone in town knew his wife, Edie, was running with Bobby Haskell, who owned the hardware store. They had been seen meetin' at the Wagon Wheel Motel, and some said they'd seen them go into Rosie Blackburn's. I don't know about that, since Rosie's is right in town and would have been too close. Anyway, Harold went home, and she wasn't there. I suspect that Harold was not as dumb as he looked, and there was too much talk for him not to know something was going on. Well, he started out looking for her. She had parked her car in back of Mrs. Weddington's garage. This was before my store was here. There was just this old house and garage here by itself. There was no way to hide her car, and Edie didn't drink, so Harold knew she wouldn't be in the bar. He took his old double-barrel shotgun from the trunk of his car and knocked on every door until he heard Edie's voice. There was only the one door to the room, so she had no way to get out. He broke down the door, shooting both barrels into the bed and into his wife and her lover. They said the buckshot splattered the whole back wall of the room. Sarah said they covered the holes with ends of tin cans and painted over them. Are they still there?"

I nodded. I had to admit I found the story intriguing in the light of day, but I knew when I was alone at night, I would remember every detail and wouldn't be able to sleep.

Mrs. Owens took a sip of Coke and, afraid of losing her audience, dove back into the story.

"Bobby Jo—that's my husband—was a deputy then. He came up here with Sheriff Potter, and he said old Mrs. Weddington and Freddy, who tended bar, had shovels and were scooping up the blood off the floor. After they cleaned up the mess, they still couldn't get the stains off the walls or the floor, so they painted it that horrible-looking red. I don't know how you stand that room. It gives me the shudders just thinking about it."

I was grateful when the dryer stopped, giving me an excuse to get away from Mrs. Owens and her stories. I would never be able to sleep in that room again without fighting the fear that I would see a disembodied soul wander through the room.

* * *

As a nurse in training, I was assigned many patients each day. We were short staffed as it was, so I took on the duties of other nurses as well as my own.

Although I had learned my lesson after Allan Spaulding died, I couldn't help but become friends with a lot of the patients—and one in particular. He was a sailor by the name of Gene Kelly, like the dancer. He lived in Shelby, Kentucky, and had taken ill while visiting friends here.

He was released from the hospital as I was getting off my shift at 4:00, and he offered me a ride.

He had a beautiful, shiny, red convertible, and the top was down. As he drove me home, I noticed Billy coming up to the field to tend to the cattle. He watched as we pulled up in front of the house. Gene noticed Billy's staring and asked me who he was. I told him he was just a boy I knew.

I was sitting in the car talking to Gene, when he invited me to a wiener roast that weekend. As he did, he reached into his glove compartment and took something out.

"Well, at least we won't have to worry about keeping warm this weekend." He smiled.

I was so naïve and dumb that I did the only thing I could do: I slapped him across the face.

"Just because I let you bring me home does not mean I'm *that* kind of girl!"

The item in his hand fell onto the seat. I thought it was a box of condoms; however, it was a box of matches. He had simply meant he would build us a campfire at the wiener roast.

Needless to say, I got out of the car, and he couldn't get out of there fast enough. I went home and sat on the front porch. I watched as Billy made his way toward me. I was so embarrassed.

He walked up on the porch and said, "I guess you'd rather go out with someone like that, huh?"

I explained everything to him, and I felt like a fool.

He was so happy that he pulled a little black box from his pocket. It was an engagement and wedding ring set he had ordered from a magazine for $10.98. He proposed right there on the front porch.

It broke my heart to do it, but I turned him down. His heart was broken, too, and he never came back to see me again or went across to the field to tend the cattle. I guess he went back home.

I was only sixteen and didn't want to be married, be pregnant every nine months, and end up living in the holler.

At the time, I guess I was still sad about me and Ed not getting married, but I realized it was all for the best.

Then came word that Billy had joined the navy, and his grandmother gave Mom his address in Rhode Island to give to me. We wrote back and forth for a while, till he got shipped overseas and we lost contact.

At least I was helping our country and doing my part for the war effort by breaking men's hearts and sending them off to the military.

* * *

Sometime after Billy left, I was walking

home from the hospital when an ambulance flew right by and stopped at the boardinghouse. I knew the driver, and when I got there, I asked what was going on.

"Hey, Virgie, I didn't know you lived here. Do you know a Mrs. Jenkins? I understand she fell down some stairs. She's eight months pregnant with twins. Do you know which apartment is hers?"

I knew the Jenkins family, but really didn't like them. Mr. Jenkins left when he discovered his wife Edna was pregnant. He said the baby wasn't his, and he was not going to support a child that wasn't.

Edna had two daughters. Elizabeth, nineteen, beautiful, spoiled, and conceited, had the disposition of a king cobra that never missed the opportunity to strike at anything that moved. Elmira, who had recently celebrated her seventeenth birthday, was indeed cut from the same bolt.

Neither of them liked the other or their own mother.

I felt Mr. Jenkins was justified in his accusation that he was not the father of his wife's unborn child—or children, as was the case.

I have, on more than one occasion, see Edna slip into or out of Bo Huffman's room in the maroon silk housecoat she wore nightly and most of the day.

It was obvious there was nothing underneath it.

Bo had been in Pikeville for months. Some said he was a shade salesman. On his second night at the apartment house—and any other time he got the opportunity—he invited me to his room, which I declined. Much to my relief, the first time I saw him leave Edna's room, his invitations stopped. I no longer had to sneak by his room at night when I got home.

They took Edna out on a stretcher, and I overheard someone say she had deliberately thrown herself down the stairs to abort her babies.

The driver called out, "Hey, Virgie, could you wait up a minute? You know Mrs. Jenkins, and we might need some help."

I wanted to tell him that I really didn't care to help her, but as a student nurse, I knew I should. And if I didn't, I would feel guilty—not to mention probably being reported to the hospital.

I stood on the porch as they lifted her into the ambulance. Her two daughters had obviously been arguing. Elmira, her hair in curlers, snapped at Elizabeth.

"I couldn't care less about your hair. I have a date with Charlie Reynolds, and I'm going to keep it." She looked at me and said, "Virgie, you go with her to the hospital. I have a date."

And so I did. She was taken back into a room and I waited. Finally, one of the nurses came out and said both babies were stillborn. She'd offered to dispose of them, but Edna had said no, she would bury them herself.

Instead, she asked me to take them home. I didn't know what to do with two dead babies, but when the nurse handed the two shoeboxes to me, I took them.

My curiosity got the best of me, and I

opened the boxes. Inside each was a beautiful, fully-formed baby, one boy and one girl. I carried the boxes with me on the eleven-mile walk home. It was dark now, and I was alone.

The boardinghouse had a family pantry with a small refrigerator. The house was dark when I got home, and I didn't know what to do with the babies, so I put them in the refrigerator. I would wait until morning to decide what to do.

Sometime during the night, one of the other tenants, Mrs. Brown, let out a bloodcurdling scream. Upon waking, I realized what had happened and ran downstairs to explain.

When I got downstairs, the refrigerator door was wide open, and Mrs. Brown was standing there, shaking.

I was able to calm her down, and I buried the babies the next morning.

White Sheets and White Knuckles

The summers were very hot in Kentucky, and I used to look forward to coming home after the long walk from the hospital, reaching into the fridge, and grabbing a cold bottle of pop.

One night, I came in late. I tried hard to be quiet, since I knew the people who had the room next to the kitchen would be asleep. I tiptoed up the porch steps and into the kitchen.

Off the kitchen was a door that led to the panty where the refrigerator was. I opened the door, got my pop, and took a long drink. Then I heard the kitchen door open.

The door had no lock or doorknob, just a hole where one had been. I heard someone talking and started to walk out, but something stopped me.

I heard someone say, "Goddamn it, Dean, we can't do the same thing we did the other night. I told you no more killing! We're gonna get ourselves caught."

Another man said, "Yeah! How long do you think we're gonna continue to get away with killing them colored bastards? I don't like them any better than you do, but we're gonna have to find another way to deal with them."

I peeped through the hole and saw Mr. and Mrs. Profitt talking to several people. I couldn't tell if they were men or women, because they were all dressed in white robes, their faces covered in what looked like white pillowcases with holes cut out for their eyes and mouths.

One of them said, “Yeah, it’ll be too dangerous, so we’d better not wear our hoods.”

They talked about how they’d actually put a man up for “execution” the week before, and I remembered hearing Sheriff Long had been found dead in the back woods. Now they were talking about shooting one sheriff each week until they “found the right one.”

Mrs. Profitt said, “Yeah, he’s been ready for execution for a long time. He’s got it comin’.”

When, I heard the scrape of chairs as the guests got up from the table, I ran upstairs and locked my door, praying I had not been overheard.

I didn’t know the full meaning of what I’d just overheard, but I’d seen the KKK before. When I was little, Daddy and I used to wander in the woods, and we caught a glimpse of those ghostly figures more than once.

I knew enough to be afraid of what they might do to me if they knew I’d seen them. The fear I had of them didn’t stop after that night, and it brought back memories of another time I’d seen the Klan in action.

At the time, we lived at Mrs. Bartlett’s boardinghouse on Ferguson Creek, across the river from Pikeville.

I was sitting on the front porch in the dark when I heard a woman screaming. My first thought was to mind my own business, so I stayed quiet and didn’t move. It was pitch-black that night, and I waited to see what the commotion was all about. Suddenly, the glow of torches lit the dark road, and I saw a group of people walking toward me.

As they passed, I saw what looked to be a man tied to a bed rail, lifted high and carried by men in white robes and hoods.

The man on the rail looked to be colored, but his skin was shiny in the yellow torch light, and he had feathers all over his body.

A group of screaming colored people followed along behind them. I didn't move a muscle, and I was terrified to make a sound, for fear they'd notice me. I didn't dare get up and go inside.

I never told another soul, because I didn't know who to trust.

Now, aside from hunger, you could add this fear to my list of worries.

Mom, The Town Whore

After hearing the horror stories about my room and the house surrounding it, I no longer felt safe at the boardinghouse, so I went back to Dad and Jenny's.

Since I'd left, they'd moved closer to town, so my walk to the hospital was shorter. Most of the hillbillies had moved out, and Dolph had died a while back, so the place was not as busy as it was before, but I didn't plan to stay too long.

Some time passed, and I hadn't seen or heard from Mom. I assumed she was still living at the boardinghouse, so I went there to see her.

A woman told me she had moved out and was living in an apartment on Jefferson Street with two other women. I went to see her and found that all three of them were prostitutes.

She didn't seem to care one way or the other that I was there and said she had a "date" at 8:00 and had to go. She simply walked off toward the railroad tracks and left me there alone in the dark.

After the whorehouse where Mom lived closed down, another one opened up down the street. Called The Rambler's Roost: Rest Haven for Men, it was directly across the street from the police station, and it was run by a woman named Mona.

Prostitution was illegal; however, it was organized and accepted by many. The girls all saw doctors on a regular basis and were tested for venereal diseases.

Pikeville was located in a dry county where

you couldn't drink alcohol, but you could buy a prostitute any night of the week.

One night I went to see her again, and she wasn't there. I figured she was out working, so I went up to her apartment to wait for her.

Jewell—now ten years old—was there, so we waited for her together, but she never came home. Neither did the other two women. I got concerned, not only about them but about us.

There was no food or money in the entire apartment.

When I went to the police department to see if they had seen her, I found out all three women were in jail. Seems they had gone to the health department for their medical checkups, and all three had VD. They were locked up for not getting it treated.

It was the 1940s, and penicillin was a new drug—a "kill or cure drug"— and it was used widely as the first cure for venereal disease.

As a nursing student, I often saw prostitutes come into the hospital to be treated for VD, only to leave without getting treatment because they were too afraid of the penicillin. Because of that, the sexually transmitted disease spread further.

The deputy let me into the jail to see Mom. I was sixteen years old and disgusted as I looked through the cell bars at my mother who was a weedmonkey, a whore. I didn't even want to talk to her. At that moment, I was ashamed to be her daughter.

When she saw me, she broke down in tears. "I'm a terrible mother! I know you're so ashamed of me."

She babbled on, and I heard Ed's name mentioned. She admitted that she'd been sleeping with him, and she knew it would hurt me so she kept quiet.

No wonder I hadn't seen him around. She said he came straight to see her when he came home on leave. She also admitted that he'd sent me several letters while in the service, and after reading them, she threw every one of them in the trash.

Why him? Why the man I loved and hoped to one day reconcile with? Anyone but him!

I didn't say a word to her, nor did I cry or get angry. I just looked at her in pure disgust and left.

This was not the first time Mom had been arrested. The first time came a few months before, and she was bold enough to call me, but didn't seem too ashamed. I was at the hospital, and the head nurse called me into her office to take an emergency phone call.

"Virgie, this is Mama, I'm in jail. Could you bring some things down here for me? That new sheriff doesn't know which side his bread is buttered on. He sent over two men to raid the Roost. Can you imagine him doing something like that? He's one of my best customers, too. You wait till I see him. I'm gonna tell him a thing or two. Oh, and before I forget, you better bring my toothbrush, toothpaste, and makeup. Looks like we're gonna be in here a while."

I didn't even bother to ask her why she was in jail; at that point, I didn't care. I hung up the phone and looked at the nurse. I hoped she hadn't heard my mother on the phone. I told her there was an emergency with my little sister, and I had to leave. She didn't look happy but agreed to sign me out with the promise that I would return later that day.

I thought about Mom's phone call. She had no perception whatsoever of my shame at being the daughter of the town whore.

After her second arrest, I decided to leave for good.

I went back to the apartment and waited with Jewell till Mom was released. I'd had enough. I wanted out of that nowhere town, and I wanted out of the life Mom and Daddy had started for me.

Those mountains were too small for me now; I couldn't breathe another minute of that hillbilly air.

I slept there so Jewell wouldn't be alone, which she said was most of the time.

The next morning, I got up and went to make Jewell some breakfast, but there was only a stale loaf of bread. We ate a few slices anyway to keep our stomachs from rumbling.

I walked over to the refrigerator, searching for some milk to ease the stomach pain that had awakened me. Doc Parsons once said it sounded like an ulcer, but when he described that as a hole in the stomach, it made me even sicker.

The milk was sour, so I poured it down the sink.

I couldn't give in to the pain, not today. I would need all my strength and courage to face telling Mom I was leaving. I didn't want it this way. I had tried many times to make her understand, but it was like talking to a child. Mom would pretend to listen, impatiently waiting for the lecture, as she called it, to end.

The results were always the same. She promised to leave prostitution as soon as Mona could find another girl. I couldn't make her understand that I could not take it anymore.

Again, I did what I did best: I ran.

I went to talk to Preacher Willis on Julius Avenue about staying with him and his family until I could leave town. Being a man of God and someone who was anchored to Christ, he said yes and took me in.

I told them up front that I would get a part-time job and pay rent every month, and it wasn't long before I got a job at the candy counter at Hobb's Five and Dime.

The Willises put up a small bed for me in their daughter's room. Sissy was not happy about sharing her room with me, but I had no plans to stay there long. Their son, Danny, was a teenage dream who played football and was popular with the girls. I had the biggest crush on him.

My chance to leave Pikeville came in the form of a letter from my Aunt Blarney, Uncle Charlie's sister. Seems her husband, Edward, had been injured in the war, and she asked me to come to their home in Washington, DC, to help care for him. I jumped at the chance.

Uncle Edward had been driving for the Bell Cab Company, but he was forced to give up his position after his injury.

The doctors had put a metal plate in his head, and the pressure of the plate would sometimes cause him to suffer from amnesia. He'd get lost, which wasn't good when he had a fare in the cab.

Sometimes he was unable to find his way back home, and Aunt Blarney would call all over the place looking for him. Once, he was found at the Veterans' Hospital in California!

Well, he had wandered off again and left her with two children, the youngest being two months old. After she found him again, she decided she needed help with him, so she contacted me.

Their life savings almost gone, she couldn't afford to hire someone to babysit and needed to go back to work at the Hot Shoppe. Her letter could not have come at a better time.

I often dreamed about and prayed for an escape from Pikeville, and this was an opportunity for me to do just that. In my dreams, however, I saw myself leaving with a tall, dark, handsome man sitting lovingly by my side, smiling at the townsfolk from a long, black, chauffeur-driven limousine. I'd wave at the peasants who had laughed at me when I was known as Virgie Hopkins, daughter of the town whore.

In exchange for a room, food, and a small allowance, I agreed to care for the children and help with Uncle Ed. Aunt Blarney sent me money for the trip. The fare was eleven dollars, but she sent thirteen.

I told Preacher Willis I was leaving, and he said he understood and wished me well. The very day I was set to leave, as I was ironing my clothes in the kitchen, in walked Danny. He pulled up a chair.

"Are you really going to Washington? I don't want you to leave."

"You wait this long to tell me?" I said.

He shuffled his feet under the table. "I know, but I've liked you for a long time."

I'd been excited about leaving until he said all that, but I knew if I passed up this opportunity to leave Kentucky, I would never get out. I would die an old, married woman with six kids strapped to my hip, hate my life, and always dream of something more. Plus, I'd already told Aunt Blarney I was coming.

"Will I ever hear from you again? Or see you?" he asked. "You hear tell of those big city guys and how they can sweep a girl off her feet."

I looked at him. I looked around at my living conditions, my home, and thought about my family and what was left of my mother. They didn't even know where I was, or if they did, they surely didn't care. I had grown up fast and had no choice but to make my own way.

I stepped outside on the porch and looked at Pikeville. I saw people living in poverty, men covered in black soot from the mines, young girls with protruding bellies and babies on their hips and at their feet.

What about Jewell and Wade? I'd been both

sister and mother to them, but I didn't even know where they were at that moment. What kind of mother was I? If I stayed, would I end up like my own mother?

I thought about Danny. What kind of life would I have with him? He'd probably die young with a lung full of coal dust or walk out in front of a train. Or maybe if he was lucky, I would have chased him off into the military and he could come back home a lost and broken man.

I made my decision. I was going to Washington.

I went back to Mom's to check on Jewell, who was alone and hungry. I fed her what little food I could find in the apartment and asked her where Mom was. She just shrugged her bony shoulders.

I don't know why, but I felt a need to tell Mom I was leaving Pikeville. I knew if I told Jewell, she would run to Mom and tell her first chance she got, but I wanted to be the one to break the news, to tell her how I really felt.

Mom did not come home that night, so I stayed with Jewell.

The pain in my stomach had gotten worse, so I went to bed early. Early morning came and Mom was still not home. I laid there but couldn't rest.

The things I had to tell Mom were whirling in my head like a carousel. I had to get up and face the day. I slipped my legs over the side of the bed onto the cold linoleum floor, trying not to wake Jewell who was sleeping beside me.

There was no reason to hurry. My train didn't leave until 11:00.

I sat in the darkness, listening to the early morning sounds: the familiar hiss of steam escaping from Lu Chan's Laundry, the thud of the overloaded washers washing away the customers' dirty secrets. Mamaw always said you could learn more about a person by looking at his laundry then you could by reading his mail.

I listened to the frantic chirping of the baby sparrows as their mother returned to her nest on the window ledge. Each time I came there, I checked their progress, watching them grow from ugly, prehistoric-looking creatures to beautiful balls of down with an appetite that forced their mother on a round-the-clock schedule of collecting food. At that moment I envied them.

I looked at Mom's empty bed. We had an understanding that I would not interfere with her personal life, but I was glad she wasn't there this morning. I wanted to put off telling her I was leaving for as long as possible.

I watched from the window as the sun cut a path through the early morning fog. I saw the rooftops of the houses and businesses, and I spotted the top half of the sign that advertised The Rambler's Roost-Rest Haven for Men.

I turned away, a tightness building again in my stomach. I reached for the sour milk, cursing my mother.

She never returned.

Leaving Pikeville

Mom found out I was leaving and was at the train station when I got there.

She clung to me, cried, and begged me not to leave her. I had not spoken to her since I saw her in jail this last time, and I wasn't any happier to see her now than I was then. I tried to break her grasp, but she got down on her hands and knees and grabbed me by the ankles, pleading with me not to get on the train.

What did she care? For the last several years, she wasn't even a mother to us. Now she was a prostitute with her own clientele to take care of, one of whom was a man I cared deeply for. What kind of woman does that to her children? To Daddy?

Daddy was no different, though, married to that little girl with one baby and another on the way. He no longer cared for me the way he once had. I missed him most of all but had lost respect for him over the years.

Mom was making a spectacle of herself, so I pulled her off her knees. "Mom, please! You're embarrassing me."

When I got on the train, she followed me up the steps and tried to snatch my old cardboard suitcase from my hands. Everyone was looking at us. Hadn't she caused me enough shame?

I finally stopped and looked at her. "Mom, I don't want to end up here. I have a chance to get out, and I'm going to take it. I don't want to end up like *you*!"

At that, her hold on me loosened, and her hands dropped from around my arms. She looked at me with the saddest face I've ever seen. Her eyes were dead with grief, and as she stepped down onto the platform, I watched as a slow Kentucky breeze gently blew her auburn hair across her face. She was still the most beautiful woman I had ever seen.

I found my seat in back. I held my suitcase in my lap until I saw the other passengers put theirs on the rack over their seat.

I had only been on a train once, when I'd been trying to escape Uncle Howard, and I'd had no luggage then. I wondered if it was obvious to the other passengers that I was a scared little girl.

I watched as the passengers boarded, fearful Mom might be among them as she made a last-ditch effort to keep me there with her. I wished the train would hurry. What was taking so long?

I closed my eyes and prayed, "Dear God, please don't let me give in and turn around and stay."

I pressed my cheek against the seat. Although its cracked surface irritated my skin, I did not move. I welcomed the pain. It made me feel less guilty about leaving a note for Mom, though I'm sure Jewell got to her before she had time to read of my departure.

Suddenly, Mom appeared at my window, banging on the glass and crying out for me.

"Please come back, Virgie! What will I do without you?" she wailed at the smudged train window which did little to muffle the sound of her cries.

I did feel guilty for abandoning her. I knew she was dependent on me to help pay her bills and buy her food, but what about me? She had leaned on me for the past several years. Who took care of me?

It was my turn for some happiness.

I didn't give in. Someone came over and took Mom by the arm, pulling her away from the platform. She was still sobbing like a baby. I watched her as the train began to move, slowly at first, and I breathed a sigh of relief as we rolled out of the station.

I felt a sense of sadness upon leaving Kentucky. As the train passed by the old, red-brick schoolhouse, I closed my eyes. I could not block out the memories of the ugly, crude-looking boys who stopped me in the hallway to ask if I would give them a "piece."

"That's all right. If you won't give me any, your mother will. I just thought I could get it from you for free," they used to say with a laugh as I walked away from them.

Once, my English teacher, Mr. Abbot, asked me to stay after school. His offer was for better grades if I'd be "nice" to him. I ran from the room, down the hall, and right past the principal, Mr. Fralin, who called out to me but I didn't stop. I always liked Mr. Fralin, and I think he understood why I chose to quit school.

I remembered Mom's response when I told her about Mr. Abbott's remarks.

She laughed and said, "Well, baby, that's what you have to put up with when you're attractive. Men like pretty girls, so learn to take advantage of it. You scratch his back, and he'll scratch yours. That's the secret to getting by in this world. A woman can get anything she wants if she plays her cards right."

The train picked up speed as we passed the billboard informing everyone that the Pension Hotel now had an elevator. I never knew why they'd spent so much money on an elevator, since the hotel had only two floors. I'd always hated that sign. It was the first thing you saw when entering Pikeville, and it was the perfect example of what a hick town Pikeville really was.

As the train snaked its way around the mountain track, I turned to look, hopefully for the last time, at the place I'd called home for most of my life.

The mountains blocked my view of the town, and the only thing visible was a massive, white cross perched on the tallest mountain overlooking Pikeville. I never knew if the cross had been put there by the KKK or by the local church as a warning to the Klan. It was something the townspeople never talked about. It just was.

The train had already rolled past the store, the mines, Ed's house. I was leaving my whole life behind. It wasn't much of a life, but it was the only one I'd ever known.

Washington, DC

It was 1945, and I was still living with Aunt Blarney and Uncle Edward in Washington, DC, on 13 ½ F Street. I loved the city. Back then there were no worries, and you could walk down the street at night and not be afraid. DC was a nice place, clean and social, like a small town.

Although the war had ended, it was still common to see soldiers in the city. In a way, it made me feel even safer.

There was a streetcar that went past the navy yard, and a ticket to take you across town would cost you ten cents.

There was a Marine barracks at 9th and G Streets, and it took up a whole block. I often sat on my front porch and listened to the music and laughter when they had their parties. They always sounded so festive, and I wondered what it would be like to be invited one day.

Although I'd been out of the hills for some time, I was still a mountain girl and had a lot to learn about the ways of the world.

One beautiful winter evening as I walked back from the store, a light snow began to fall, glistening like tiny, silver diamonds under the glow of the streetlights.

I didn't notice the two GIs behind me until one of them said, "Hi there! May I carry your groceries?"

I turned to see two handsome men in uniform.

I said no thank you and kept walking. Back then, you didn't have to be afraid of people, so when they asked me where I lived, I told them.

The one who said his name was Bob mentioned that he lived right across the street from me and pointed to his house. The other one, Grant, said nothing.

Bob said they were home on leave from the air force and were about to be shipped overseas to Germany to a replacement depot. They were shipping soldiers out so others could come home. But before they left, they were planning a trip to Ogden, Utah.

I must have been attractive to them, with my southern accent and naïve charm. When we reached my house, they asked to come in. I told them no, that I didn't know them well enough, so they left.

An hour later, there was a knock on my door. It was Grant, who admitted that he lived just around the corner. It was obvious that he wanted to come in, but I was in the middle of making chili, which I had never done before, and I really didn't want to be bothered.

"Something smells really good. What are you cooking," he asked.

"Chili, but it probably won't turn out too good. I'm trying out a new recipe."

I smiled and promised to make him some when I got to know him better. He just stood there in the cold in his starched air force uniform, his big, blue eyes piercing me like daggers. Suddenly, I realized how silly I was being and invited him in.

Grant ate every bite of his chili. He was

either starving or trying hard to impress me, because it really wasn't too tasty. I'd apparently put too much cayenne pepper in it, but it didn't seem to stop him.

After dinner, we went into the living room to talk. He was a nice enough man, but if I'd been given a choice, I'd have chosen Bob over Grant any day. So, I asked where Bob was, hoping Grant would take the hint. I was relieved when he left less than ten minutes later.

The next day was Saturday, and before noon, Grant had come back to the house to see me. Aunt Blarney and the kids were home, and Grant invited us all to Glen Echo amusement park.

I asked about Bob again, and Grant said he'd been invited to join us but had other plans. I enjoyed the rides, shopping, and sampling the food, but I couldn't stop thinking about Bob.

I was now seventeen and Grant was nineteen. I had come to DC to find myself and to make my own way, so when he asked me out to dinner, I was uneasy. I wasn't interested in him at all, but I put my fears aside and said yes to the dinner date. After all, he'd been especially nice to me. Just as we headed out to catch the street car, Bob ran across the street.

"Hi, Bob," I said as he fell into step beside us. "We're going to grab a bit to eat. Want to join us?"

"I'd love to," he replied.

I hope Bob didn't see the look Grant gave him as he linked his arm through mine. Grant obviously minded the intrusion, though I was happy about it.

The next day, the three of us spent most of the day together. I enjoyed Bob's company more and more as I got to know him.

When Grant showed up alone the following day, I was disappointed, but it was obvious he had something on his mind. He took a photo from his pocket and handed it to me.

"Don't you think you look like her?" he said.

Although the photo of the young girl was creased and taken at a distance, I agreed we could be sisters.

Seems the girl, June, was his girlfriend. When he came home on leave from Biloxi, Mississippi, he bought an engagement and wedding ring set and asked her to marry him.

I was glad to hear he was already taken, since I wanted to be with Bob anyway.

But there was more. He said he'd told all his friends and family about the girl and bragged on the fact that she was going to say yes. But when he went to her mother's house to see her and propose, her mother said she was in the hospital, in the maternity ward. Grant knew he'd been away too long for the baby to be his, and June admitted that the baby belonged to a mutual friend of theirs.

Grant still wanted to marry her, but she turned him down.

"It was so embarrassing," he said as he stuffed the photo back in his pocket. "I have a favor to ask you. I'll understand if you say no . . . but . . . would you consider marrying me? It would kill me to have to tell the guys the truth."

I met Grant on the tenth of December, and on December seventeenth I became his wife.

I didn't love him, but he was a kind man, and I looked at him as a way out of the life that awaited me back home.

I knew I never wanted to go back to Kentucky and marry one of the boys in the hills or be a coal miner's widow. Now I'd be the wife of a soldier, and I would never have to go back to Pikeville again.

As he'd told me when we met, Grant had planned a trip to Utah before being shipped to Germany. I'd never been far from home, and I found the plane ride exciting. But I was unprepared for the weather in Salt Lake City.

It had to be the coldest place on earth! Even the moisture in my nostrils froze! I'd never liked the cold, and although it was a beautiful city, I had no immediate plans to return.

After we got back, Grant went to Germany, and I was sent to live with his mother, Ada. She lived in a beautiful seaside home at Point Lookout, Maryland. I adored her and her spacious home with its windows looking out over the ocean. I spent every day on the beach.

Grant was gone for two years. I spent the time taking secretarial courses and worked hard to get rid of my southern accent.

I read every book I could find on bettering myself and learning to speak correctly. I listened to tapes on grammar and how to pronounce words without my accent. I wanted to get as far away from

Kentucky and my past as possible.

I had never learned how to drive, so Grant taught me before he went overseas.

My parallel parking left much to be desired, so he used matchboxes as cars to show me how to do it . . . and it worked!

I got my driver's license at seventeen and was able to drive into DC for classes.

The Return to Pikeville

I'd been gone for almost a year and decided to go back to Kentucky for a visit. It wasn't a visit in the usual sense, however. It was to show off. I wanted to show the people there how I'd been to the big city and was now a polished adult. I bought the prettiest fuchsia suit and hat to wear. I was so above my raisin'!

The train pulled into Pikeville, and I noticed two benches on the platform—one marked Whites Only and the other Coloreds Only. Even the bathrooms were segregated! Some things had not changed.

I got off the train, and who did I run into but Ed Adkins. I thought about how he'd come to Tennessee to bring me home to marry him. I wondered how different my life would be if we had married like we'd planned. But then I thought about him being with Mom, and my stomach turned.

We sat in the station for a bit to catch up. Ed told me how he'd joined the navy after my uncle turned him away that night in Tennessee.

He'd been upset and unsure about what to do with his life. I told him about all the letters I'd written him and how I'd worked hard to save enough money to come home to him only to find him gone when I arrived.

He looked at me funny and said, "Really? I didn't know you did that. No one ever told me."

He said he was married now and had three kids, but he wasn't happy in the marriage.

I wasn't really interested in the details, but he was in a talking mood. Well, he'd come home on leave with a friend of his from boot camp, a guy from Wheelwright, a little area in Pike County. He wanted to show his friend around, and they ended up in a bar and got drunk. He met his friend's sister and doesn't remember much else about the evening, but he woke up in a motel room, hungover, with the girl in bed next to him. He got up to leave while she was asleep, put some money on the nightstand, and opened the door.

Suddenly she woke up, looked at the money, and started yelling.

"Do you think I'm some kind of whore or something?"

Ed told her he didn't remember the night before, but he had to go.

"Honey, you ain't going nowhere," she said as she reached into her purse and pulled out a marriage license.

I didn't believe a word of it. And honestly, at that point in my life, I didn't care.

When Ed finished his story, he asked if I would consider seeing him again. I declined. After all, he was a married man. I didn't mention what Mom had told me. Maybe she just told me that to hurt me, but maybe she was telling the truth.

I asked him if he knew where Mom was, and he said she was living at the Pension Hotel. I really didn't have anything else to say to him. I just wanted to find Mom.

I went to her room, a tiny efficiency, and I was happy to find Jewell there with her. Wade was there, too, but had his own room. He'd found a job at the ice house in town.

I told Mom I could stay for a while. While I was there, I took ill and had to have my appendix taken out. I asked Mom to come to the hospital with me, since I'd never had surgery before, and the whole idea scared me. She had other plans, so I asked Jewell if she could come. She told me she couldn't because she had an important date that night.

Seems she was still a virgin and had big plans to go "all the way" with her latest boyfriend. She never did come to the hospital. No one did.

I had my surgery and never saw Mom or Jewell after I got out, so I got on the train and went back to Washington.

I never even saw Daddy or any of them on the trip. I don't know if they knew I was even in town.

Married Life

When Grant came home, we settled into a fairly normal life as husband and wife. After the last trip, I decided to never go back to Pikeville again.

I was raised not to sit around the house, so I took on temporary jobs, hoping one would turn into something full time. I felt guilty that Grant was working and paying all the bills, and I wanted to contribute in some way.

We'd been together for several years, and I was surprised how well we got along, considering we'd only known each other for seven days before we married. We even looked alike and were often mistaken for brother and sister.

Grant got transferred to Mesa, Arizona, where we lived for several years. I loved the desert, and never wanted to return to the city, but our life was waiting for us back in DC.

Once back there, I got a job as a typesetter with the *Washington Times-Herald*. I enjoyed typing letters to the editor and weather reports, and being in the hub of the information world.

Another woman who worked there was Jacqueline Bouvier. She was the "Inquiring Camera Girl" and earned $42.50 a week. Her job was to photograph and interview local citizens, asking one question each day. Her first interview was with Pat Nixon, and others included Vice President Nixon and Senator John F. Kennedy. I never spoke to her, though. She just flitted in and out of the office with her camera in hand. She was dainty and beautiful and had the air of grace around her. She looked like a woman who was destined for something great.

One of her last assignments was to cover Queen Elizabeth's 1953 coronation. She left the newspaper to marry JFK in 1953.

* * *

I wanted to be a mother. As a young child, when I was asked what I wanted to be when I grew up, my response was always the same: a grandmother.

It was 1953, and we'd been married eight years. I wondered why I'd never gotten pregnant, and Grant finally admitted to me that he was sterile. He had contracted German measles as a child, and he'd been told then that he would never be able to father a child. I was devastated.

How could he have kept something like that from me? I'd talked often about wanting children and envied my friends who were mothers. But I blamed myself for marrying a man I'd only known a week. I threatened to leave him, and he brought up adoption. I wanted to be a mother, no matter if it was to my own biological child or someone else's who needed me, so we started asking around.

Jewell, who had since left Kentucky and was living in Washington as well, told me about a friend of hers at work who was pregnant and planned to put the baby up for adoption.

Her name was Nadine, and she had given birth to several children—I think at last count there were nine—and she'd given them all away.

We met and she approved of us. In 1954,

she gave birth to a beautiful little girl who was adopted right into our arms and into our life. We named her Lydia. I fell in love with her at first sight and loved being a mother.

According to the law, Nadine had one full year to change her mind, and although the baby could live with us, she was allowed full visitation rights. Each time she came to visit, I was terrified she would take the baby and run, but she never did. She looked at the baby with no more feeling than if she was looking at a doll.

She didn't want her, plain and simple.

* * *

Grant left the air force and fulfilled his dream of opening a flower nursery in a suburb of Washington. The nursery was operated from our home, and although I loved working with the plants and flowers, something was missing from my life. I knew I'd rushed into things with Grant. I'd grown to care for him, but love was not a word I'd use to describe my feelings for him.

I'd had plenty of opportunities to be with other men, but I would never go the route Mom had taken and put my husband and child through that. I wanted a different kind of life than the one I'd left years ago.

Often Grant and I would go to cocktail parties, and other women thought we were related. On one such occasion, we had gone out for the evening, leaving Lydia with Jewell. A lovely young woman at the table with us was flirting openly with

Grant. He made no effort to mention I was his wife, so I chose not to, either. Mamaw always said, “if you let a man talk long enough, he’ll hang himself with his own tongue.”

When I politely excused myself to go to the ladies room, she followed.

“Wow! That brother of yours sure is a dream!” She gushed.

I just smiled and said, “Yes, I can tell he likes you, too. Why don’t you ask him for his number?”

“Don’t you think that would be too bold?”

“No, he likes a woman who knows what she wants. Go ahead, ask him.”

As we returned to the table, I saw a funny look on Grant’s face. He thought we gals had gone off for a catfight in the powder room. But I knew a better way to handle this.

The young woman moved her chair closer to Grant’s, and he began to fidget. She played with his hair and laid on the charm thick as molasses, but he said nothing about me being his wife. Finally, she made her move.

“Your sister and I were just chatting about you in the ladies’ room,” she said, leaning in close. “She said you were interested. Maybe you’d like to take me out sometime?”

Somehow I managed not to laugh, but the look on Grant’s face made it pretty darn hard. He said nothing, just got up, took my arm, and led me from the room. In the car, he let me have it.

“How could you let that woman think I was

your brother?"

I just smiled. "How could you?"

We rode home in silence.

We got into the routine of raising Lydia and running our nursery. I had not been back to Kentucky since the last time, and although I missed Daddy, I knew things would never be the same. Jewell kept in touch with him, and she told me how he and Jenny had gone on to have six children, three boys and three girls.

Then Daddy divorced her in 1953 and married another woman named Laverne. They had three daughters together. I knew I would never go back to being his honey girl after all that.

Jewell kept tabs on Mom, too. She was still living in the boardinghouse and entertaining men, as she called it. Jewell said that although she was no longer a young woman, her beauty had not escaped her.

When Lydia was a year old, I came to an important decision. Though I loved her more than life itself, I did not love Grant, and I was tired of living a lie.

He knew we had entered into a marriage of convenience, a marriage based on a lie. A marriage that I was promised would be over once I had done my "duty" and helped Grant save face with his friends and family. But he refused to divorce me.

I had matured many years since that December day, and I was no longer a naïve seventeen-year-old. I was now twenty-six and wanted more out of life, so I left him.

Everyone advised me to leave Lydia behind. Even Jewell said Grant was better equipped to give her a good life, more financially stable and secure. I was still working at the newspaper and worked part-time at the nursery on weekends.

"Do what's best for her," I was told. "Leave her with her father."

How I wish I had listened to my heart instead of them! I stayed away for a year, and with every passing day, my heart broke more. When I returned, she didn't know me. I was Mom all over again. What had I done to my child? I hated myself and begged this innocent little girl to forgive me.

I am a firm believer that a child is much better off with one happy parent then two unhappy ones, and I didn't want Lydia raised in an environment where love between her parents did not exist. I believed Grant loved me passionately, but one love for two hearts is not enough.

I continued to live the lie until 1957, when I moved into my own apartment and took the baby with me. It was difficult, but I had no choice. I got help from my friends, and I found a reliable young girl to watch Lydia while I was at work.

Grant called me nonstop and tormented me daily with presents and visits and affirmations of his love. Didn't he get it? I never loved him, and after twelve years, I knew I never would.

I admit I was lonely and scared, but it wasn't the first time I'd been on my own and responsible for a baby. I could have given up, packed up, and moved back to Kentucky, but I chose not to.

* * *

It was 1958, and I was still working at the newspaper and making a decent living. Mom had remarried, and according to Jewell, Clyde was good to her. Mom also suffered irreparable damage to her brain and nervous system from years of untreated syphilis.

Jewell had married a nice man, Donald, who was an alcoholic. She was hard on him, which made him drink even more. I often said I don't know how he kept from killing her. They had a child together, a little girl named Eve.

Mom and Clyde moved up from Kentucky and got a house a few blocks down from Jewell and her family. While Jewell was at work, Mom would come over and babysit Eve. Well, after a while, Jewell said Mom began acting strange and saying bizarre things, and eventually she and Clyde went back to Kentucky.

It wasn't long before Mom called and asked Jewell if she could come and stay with her and Donald. It was obvious that Mom was far from well. She began talking to herself and to the television and saying things no one could understand.

One time, Mom asked Jewell to look at the back of her head, because she thought her brains were spilling out.

Jewell called me and Wade and asked for our help. Jewell was already dealing with her own demons and was seeing a psychiatrist, so she sought his advice as well.

I didn't believe Jewell and her claims that Mom was going insane.

I knew she'd been different when she came back home to us years before.

I knew she was suffering from the effects of untreated syphilis; however, I could not wrap my head around the fact that Mom might be losing it all together.

I also disagreed with the tactics Jewell used to get Mom help. But Wade and I had families of our own, and though we didn't believe Mom was insane, we really didn't know how to help her. Jewell's psychiatrist and a colleague of his came to her apartment to speak to Mom.

They told Jewell not to be home when they arrived. Mom, being childlike and vulnerable, let them into the apartment.

They chatted for a while. When the doctors asked Mom if she wanted to go for a drive with them, she naively said yes.

They drove her to the state mental hospital, where she was committed and spent the next three months.

How cruel and inhumane to ambush her like that and not even be there to comfort her and explain to her what was going on. As much as I'd hated her in the past, Mom did not deserve that.

I never forgave Jewell for treating our mother that way.

After being released from the hospital, Mom was sent back to live with Jewell.

She was given strong medicine to take, but

according to Jewell, she would flush it down the toilet every chance she got, certain Jewell was trying to poison her with the pills.

The Single Life

I loved working for the newspaper but never more so than the day they hired a new photojournalist named Jim Edwards. He was tall, dreamy, and looked like Gregory Peck. It wasn't long until we were working together. I volunteered to work late, weekends, whatever it took to be near him.

Soon after we met, we began dating. I was still legally married to Grant, and although the divorce was pending, I felt guilty for wanting to date Jim. He was also a little on the rough side.

He had a James Dean persona and rode a motorcycle to work, drank, wore a leather jacket, and was not the type of guy you took home to meet your parents. But I was drawn to him, and I knew he felt the same way. He fell in love with Lydia, and I thought there might be a future for us.

At the same time, I was bombarded with calls and letters from Grant, and I was torn between being an unhappy wife or a happy single parent.

It was hard enough to be a single mother, but back in the '50s, it was even more so. We didn't have the resources many single mothers have today, and relying on a man to help carry the load was quite appealing.

But I was strong and knew what I had come from. I had clawed my way out of those mountains, escaping a distant father and his thirteen other children, a mother who was the town whore, and "uncles" trying to get into my pants left and right. I had come a long way on my own, and I was not looking back.

Grant tried his best to wear me down, but he could not. I was falling in love with Jim and no longer looked at Grant as my husband.

I didn't mean to play dirty, but during the divorce proceedings I used the information about Grant withholding the fact that he was sterile. Although we'd adopted Lydia, I still wanted a child of my own.

The divorce was granted.

I threw myself into a full-blown relationship with Jim, but at times it was rocky. I needed stability in my life and a man who would provide that type of security for me.

I had seen enough upheaval and wanted to lay roots somewhere with someone I loved. But I wasn't looking for another husband just yet. I didn't want the pressure of another marriage and had no plans to jump into any fires after just leaving the frying pan.

I was drawn to Jim and his rebel-like lifestyle, but in the back of my mind, I wondered if he'd ever be able to offer the stability I needed. His drinking had become a problem. He wasn't a drunk, but when we went out, he would have too much to drink and end up getting tipsy.

And there were times when he "forgot" to show up for a date, choosing to get drunk with his friends, even though we'd made plans and I'd found a babysitter. Other times he'd be late and already had a few drinks under his belt when he came to get me. I didn't like to be around sloppy drinkers, so the evening was ruined for me before it even began.

Well, the final straw came one night when we'd made plans for a special evening, and Jim didn't show up. Although he'd done it before, this time I'd had enough. I waited over an hour and then went to his house.

His brother, Ray, answered the door and said Jim wasn't there. He could see by my dress that we'd made plans but didn't seem surprised that his brother had stood me up.

He invited me in and we talked for a bit. "You look mighty nice tonight, Virgie," he said. "Seems like a shame to let that pretty dress go to waste. Would you do me the honor of going out to dinner with me instead?"

"Yes, I'd like that, Ray."

I knew I'd made a mistake the moment I said it. I wasn't interested in him in a romantic way, but I was miffed at Jim. Besides, I was all dressed up, and I was hungry.

We had a nice time at dinner and then returned to the house to see if Jim had arrived. When we pulled in, Jim was in the driveway on his motorcycle. The look he gave me said it all. I thanked Ray for dinner and walked over to Jim.

"Where have you been, Jim? We had plans." I could smell the alcohol as I got close to him. "This isn't what you think. When I came over here all dressed up and you weren't here, Ray was nice enough to take me to dinner. That's all it was."

"So you go out with my brother instead?" His words were slurred.

"No, we didn't go out. It wasn't a date."

"Well, I know I'm late picking you up sometimes, and I know I drink a little and you don't like that, but I had a good excuse tonight." He swayed as he tried to hold up his motorcycle.

He reached into his coat pocket and pulled out a little black box. I gasped as I slowly reached for it. When he jerked it back, I was stunned.

"Go ahead, be with my brother!" He got off the bike and staggered back into the house.

I went home and cried myself to sleep.

How could I have been so stupid?

A few months went by, and Jim would no longer talk to me at work. I tried several times to explain to him that nothing had happened between Ray and me, but he refused to listen. I found out years later that Ray told him we'd slept together that night, but nothing could have been further from the truth. Jim and I hadn't even slept together; did he think I was going to sleep with his brother? I was not my mother!

* * *

I left the newspaper in 1958 and went to work as a bookkeeper for a local firm.

One of our clients was Willard Scott, who at the time was Bozo the Clown. He was nice and would come into the office from time to time and even offered me two tickets to the show so I could take Lydia. I was anxious to go, but she came down with the measles and we were unable to attend a taping.

After Jim, I began going out with friends again. The romantic harassment from Grant had stopped, Jim no longer spoke to me, and I was starting to feel pretty lonely.

Lydia was now four years old and a little brunette beauty. Grant and I had set up visitation, and it all seemed to fall into place nicely.

One day after visiting her father, Lydia came home and said her "pee pee" hurt. I took a look. The area was red, and she said it hurt to touch it. I asked her if something had happened to her at her father's. At first, she didn't answer.

I didn't suspect Grant of touching her that way; however, after the childhood I'd survived, I found it hard to trust anyone, especially a man.

Well, Lydia finally began to talk and told me her daddy had gone out and left her with the neighbor man.

"He tried to put his thing inside my thing," she whispered, "but it didn't fit. It was too big."

I took her straight to Jewell's and drove to Grant's house. When I got there, Grant was in the front yard talking to the neighbor. I pushed the gas pedal down as hard as I could and chased them through the yard with my car. Both men jumped out of the way, yelling at me to stop.

I cornered the child molester up against the tree and pinned him with my car.

As I got out, Grant ran over to me, accusing me of going insane. I told him what Lydia had said, and much to my surprise, he didn't believe me or her.

With the screaming man still pinned, I went inside and called the police. They came and arrested him on suspicion of child abuse. To make a long story short, we ended up going to trial.

There was evidence to prove the neighbor had been abusing other little girls in the neighborhood, and he was sent to jail.

Grant continued his friendship with the man until the day he went to jail and never did believe his own daughter's story.

In fact, he actually apologized to the man for my behavior!

The Frenchman and his Mother

It was 1958, and I had gone to a cocktail party with friends. Lydia was at her father's that weekend, and although I loved her, I enjoyed getting out with friends when I could.

One of my friends had been telling me about this man she knew from work. She said he was a charming, handsome Frenchman—thirty-two, single, and very available—who was the catch of the city! Born and raised in Canada, he'd moved to the states as a young man.

Although he sounded interesting, I wasn't sure I was ready to start dating again. I still loved Jim, and even though Grant had given up trying to reconcile, I could tell he still loved me every time I dropped Lydia off for her visits.

But I was lonely, so we arranged to meet. At first glance, I thought he was gay! He was handsome and had a tiny moustache perched on his upper lip. He had a slight French accent and the best sense of humor of anyone I'd ever met. Much to my chagrin, we hit it off.

Maurice was an only child and had lost his father a few years before. His father, a World War I veteran, had been poisoned by mustard gas and died a horrible death. His mother was now living with her brother who raised homing pigeons in New England.

I liked Maurice but was not really looking to get serious with anyone at that time. Plus, I found him slightly irritating. When I first met him and said his name, he quickly corrected my French and told me I should remember to roll the *R* when I said it. He laughed when he said it, but I didn't think he was joking.

Maurice was aggressive, and he didn't seem to understand that I was recently divorced and not ready to jump into anything. He told me up front that he was ready to settle down and start a family.

He was a real charmer who told me that when he met me, he was actually living with thirteen other women. Well, I found out later that he'd been living in an apartment building, and there were thirteen women living there . . . in their own apartments.

He lavished me with stories about growing up in Canada and how when he came to the states, he couldn't speak English. His family had moved to Vermont, and he was teased constantly for not knowing the language. He grew up in the Catholic church and was sent to parochial school. He became an altar boy but despised the nuns there.

He went on to college in Rhode Island, where he received a degree in English and became self-taught in nine languages, including sign language. Not only could he speak these other languages, but he could read and write them as well. Needless to say, I was impressed.

He was a talented musician, too, and played every instrument I ever saw him touch. He would delight our friends at parties with his rambunctious piano playing and sing-a-longs.

When he sang in French, my heart would melt. As an accomplished pianist, he insisted that the reason he played so well was the constant knuckle beatings (with rulers) he received from the nuns when he'd been learning to play.

He also said they gave the boys more severe beatings, making them lie down on their stomachs on the stairs while they beat them.

I didn't know whether or not to believe him but thought he might be telling the truth when he admitted that as a child, he had set the school on fire and tried to burn it down.

After several months of dating, he began to wear me down, and I found I actually liked his company. We'd been dating for two years when we stumbled upon the opportunity to purchase a farm in West Virginia. It was a beautiful place with 235 acres, an old farmhouse, several outbuildings and barns, two mountains, a creek, and a family cemetery.

We'd been on one of our weekend day trips and had driven up to Sleepy Creek, a remote area in West Virginia. We were walking around an old country store when we overheard a man talking loudly to the clerk. He was complaining and going on and on about his ungrateful children.

"Well, I ought to sell the whole goddamn place for nothing, and they won't get anything from me. They can't even wait till I'm dead and buried to start fighting over what's not even theirs yet!"

Maurice's ears perked up. He approached the man and told him we were looking to buy some property and asked was he seriously interested in selling. Well, we caught him in the right frame of mind, I guess, because he sold us the entire farm for $4,000.

I was falling in love with this crazy Frenchmen and that scared me. I really wasn't sure I even knew what falling in love felt like, but this felt right.

Then to complicate things, Jim called me again, and I often caught him sitting outside my apartment on his motorcycle.

Our conversations were usually the same: he was drunk and wanted to know what had happened with his brother. After repeatedly telling him nothing had happened, an argument would ensue, and he would accuse me of lying. Again.

I was so confused. I had Jim outside my window, Maurice in my apartment, and Grant on the phone with some excuse for calling me almost every night. I thought about the three men: Jim was a wild, reckless, bad boy who would probably break my heart. Grant was a good man but weak in character, and although he never hurt me, I didn't love him and was glad we had divorced. Maurice was stable, a good man who would probably give me a good life.

So, when Maurice proposed to me, I said yes, and on July 30, 1960, we were married.

I was in love this time and looked forward to a happy life with him.

His mother, however, did not approve of a divorced woman marrying her Catholic son. Angelina was a tough cookie to crack; she had a stone wall around her a mile thick. She spoke very little English, and when she did, I could only understand my name. Funny, it was always followed by a sharp word spoken in French.

She said my divorce from Grant was not recognized by the church, and by the laws of God, I was still married. She couldn't bear the idea that her son had married an adulteress.

She told me, "I will like you as long as my son likes you."

Well, that was not the case. She even approached Maurice on our wedding day and insisted she accompany us on our honeymoon to "keep an eye on me." According to her, her father had done the same on her honeymoon.

I had never spoken a harsh word to him about his mother or about anything, for that matter, but I turned to him and said, "This is where they separate the men from the boys. If you allow your mother to go with us on our honeymoon, this will be the shortest marriage in history."

Needless to say, she took the train back to New England, explaining that she only wanted to ride as far as Rhode Island since we were going to Canada anyway.

Maurice tried to defend her. He explained that she'd once been a lively, vibrant woman who wanted to be an actress.

Back then, a decent woman did not have aspirations of the stage, and her father forbade her from pursuing her dream.

She was a woman of faith and wanted a large family, as was expected of devout Catholics back in those days. But Maurice had been a twelve-pound baby, and her doctor felt it was too dangerous for her to get pregnant again. She was told she should never have any more children.

At that thought, one would think she would have cherished the son she had, but instead she dressed him up like a girl part of the time and a little boy the other half. That way, in her mind, she had more children. It was weird, to say the least.

As a mother, I understood her anguish at not having more children, but I was not to blame for that fact. She took out her bitterness on everyone and was envious of anyone who still had their youth and beauty.

Maurice told me animated stories of the wild parties his parents threw, and at that time they were considered quite risqué. They would invite other couples to their home to play cards and then send Maurice outside.

Curiosity would get the best of him, and he would peek inside the windows to see them all running around the room in their underwear!

Angelina also had a keen interest in the occult and actually owned her own Ouija board and Tarot cards.

Wheaton, Maryland

After returning from our honeymoon, Maurice and I bought a two-story brick colonial house in Wheaton, a suburb of Washington, DC. He'd been working for the railroad and had recently taken a job as a private investigator with the welfare department.

His hours were late, and I often went to bed alone, but he was always there in the morning when I got up. The money was good, and he was a good provider. I looked forward to having a family one day.

Maurice often came home with horror stories about waiting outside windows in the roughest part of town as rats crawled over his feet. I was constantly worried about him, but he assured me he was safe.

He had to investigate people to make sure women who were filing for welfare did not have a man living in the home and supporting them, which would have been considered welfare fraud.

When we moved to Wheaton, Lydia remained behind with her father. She was in school and at the age where she wanted to be with her friends. Changing schools would have been difficult for her.

Besides, Maurice had never accepted Lydia as his daughter, and often times he was cruel to her. Although not physically abusive, he was selfish with "his" things and "his" house . . . and even "his" sidewalk. His mother did not accept or acknowledge

Lydia, either.

Maurice and I wanted children of our own, but it didn't happen. After consulting a fertility doctor, we both took daily shots to raise our chances of being able to conceive.

I was always told that when you stopped putting pressure on yourself, relax, and quit trying to have a baby, that is when it will happen.

It didn't help that Angelina kept referring to me as a barren, scorned woman. She was certain we could not conceive because God was punishing her beloved son for marrying a divorced woman.

After four years of trying and taking shots, I was afraid it would never happen. I stopped trying and left it up to God whether or not we were to be parents. If we were being punished, we had suffered long enough.

Finally I got pregnant, and in 1964, Rebecca was born. Maurice was an exceptional father, very hands-on and loving. He fell in love with that curly-blonde-haired beauty the moment he laid eyes on her.

As I lay in the hospital, moments after giving birth, I blurted out, "I want another one!"

I was thirty-five years old, and as I listened to the younger women moaning and groaning about the pain of childbirth, all I could think was, "We did it! Now let's do it again."

My doctor was upset that I'd gotten pregnant in the first place. He said a woman my age was too old to get pregnant, and if I got pregnant again, he would drop me as a patient. True to his word, when our son, Gregory, was born fourteen months later, another doctor delivered him.

Rebecca was a lovely baby and very talkative. I swear I heard her talking in my womb before she was born. It sounded like a kitten purring. Big green eyes and a head full of blonde ringlets, she was Daddy's little girl from the start.

Gregory was born at eight months but weighed in at a healthy seven pounds. Blue eyes like mine and a towhead like his sister, our family was now complete.

Maurice had asked his mother to come down from New England to help with the baby. She was not set to come until July, but the baby was born early. This, she said, was my fault. She came anyway and grumbled about the change in plans.

Maurice got me home and settled, and although Angelina and I didn't get along, I was grateful for her help.

Rebecca was fourteen months old and an energetic handful. I now had a newborn to deal with, and on top of that, the hospital had given me a saddle block—a spinal nerve block to help me through childbirth—and I was unable to walk up and down the stairs without assistance, so Angelina's help was greatly needed.

After Maurice got me situated, he returned to work, knowing his mother would be there to help me. A few minutes after he left, I heard her on the phone downstairs. The children were asleep, and I was in need of rest as well.

I heard her come upstairs and go into her room. I called out for her, but she didn't answer. A few minutes later, I heard her footsteps on the stairs and a car horn out front. I managed to crawl out of bed and onto the floor and got myself down the hallway to the top of the stairs.

The front door was wide open, a cab driver was standing there with a suitcase, and Angelina was hurrying out the door.

I called out to her, which woke the children, but she slammed the door shut behind her without a word.

I sat at the top of the steps and bawled.

Before we married, Maurice told me what he expected from a wife. He did not want her to work. She was to stay at home and raise "his" children. He would be the provider, the bread winner, and the wife was to cook and take care of the house.

At the time, I didn't know if this was the way all wives were expected to be or if he just wanted to be in control.

I had been cooking, cleaning, and caring for children most of my life, but I was also accustomed to working and carrying my own weight. I agreed to his terms, but I knew down the road I'd want to get involved in something that would bring in extra income.

Although Maurice was a good father, his work schedule complicated things.

As I was set to go off to bed, he would come home and wake up the children. They were "his children," he said, and he hadn't seen them all day and wanted to play with them.

Once they were good and awake and ready for play, he would go to bed, and I would be up half the night with them. I got little sleep, as they were up and raring to go first thing in the morning.

Then I would feed them, feed Maurice, do the laundry, iron and starch his shirts, and clean the house. I was exhausted all the time, no end in sight.

Lydia would come over on the weekends, and Maurice hated the fact that I drove to her father's to get her. He never let me forget I was once married to another man and that Lydia was not his daughter . . . and not really mine, either.

I loved Maurice, but he changed once we had children. He idolized them but was different toward me. Although I never resented them or his love for them, I felt lonely and confused most of the time. Before we had children, he was a devilishly sexy, quite amorous man. But after I gave birth to his daughter, he changed toward me.

I was told by some female friends that Catholic men suffered from a Madonna-Whore Complex. They may find a woman sexually attractive, but once she gives birth, she is now a mother, which is sacred.

The woman is thrown into a completely different category.

I wasn't sure it explained our situation, and I didn't understand that way of thinking. I had not been brought up in church like Maurice had been. Occasionally Mom would take us to the Methodist Church or the whites-only church, but I never really got anything out of it.

I would pray that my life would improve, and I would be loved one day, and although those things came true, it sure took a while.

Mom said sometimes when you ask God for something, His answer is “not now.” She said He always hears you, and your prayers do not get ignored, but all things happen in His time, not ours.

No Escape

I tried hard to escape my life and family in Kentucky, but it had a way of finding me anyway. Wade and his family had moved to Ohio.

He and his wife, Betty, had five children. Betty was a girl we used to play with as children back in Pikeville.

I was surprised when he married her, though, because we all thought she was colored. The story in Pikeville was that her mother, a white woman, had been sneaking around with a colored man.

When she was born, there was no doubt she was his child. Her mother was attacked one night, and her throat was slit from ear to ear. Although she survived, she carried a long, ugly scar around her neck for the rest of her life.

Wade contacted me one day and said he and Betty had lost their youngest daughter at a year old. She was found dead in her crib. I was heartbroken for him and could feel his pain over the phone.

He said he'd never asked his family for anything, but would I please send him some money to help with the burial. Jewell planned to go to Ohio to see them, and she offered to take the money up with her and give it to Wade. I still harbored resentment toward Jewell for having Mom committed.

We had never been close like Wade and I, but she was my sister and I wanted to love and trust her.

Years later, Wade mentioned how upset he'd been with me for not sending him the money he'd requested. I assured him that I'd given the money to Jewell to bring to him. He didn't believe me and said it had taken a lot for him to ask me for help, and then I let him down.

I confronted Jewell about it, and she admitted she'd used the money to make a payment on an end table she'd bought on loan from the furniture store.

While I was dealing with my own personal issues, I had to put up with Jewell and her constant calls about Mom.

The untreated syphilis had destroyed her mind, and Jewell could not cope with her. Mom's husband, Clyde, had passed away in Kentucky, and she was now living with Jewell and her family full time.

She said Mom had gone insane and would not take her medicine. She'd been legally blind her whole life, but her untreated venereal disease had caused her eyesight to worsen, and she could not read the labels herself. She did not believe Jewell, who said the pills were going to help her.

I had known for years that Jewell had her own mental health issues and was on and off a psychiatrist's couch for years. Sadly, that mental illness trickled down to her daughter, Eve.

Jewell's long-suffering husband, Donald, had turned into a raging alcoholic just to be able to live with her and their daughter.

Although Jewell constantly complained about Mom, I was powerless to help her. What could I do? She had invited Mom to live with them, and I certainly did not want her to live with us. I was now an adult, but an adult who had narrowly escaped a nightmarish childhood and could not—would not—forgive Mom for what she had done to us.

Yes, she was mentally ill and partially blind, and there was a part of me that pitied her; she was, in fact, still my mother. But the other side of me said to hell with her. She'd made her bed, so she could lie in it. Alone.

Besides, I was dealing with my own issues on the home front. Maurice had a raging temper. He was wonderful to the children, but he seemed angry with me all the time.

I had done nothing but try to be a good wife and mother to his children, so I couldn't understand his brutality to me.

Maurice's hours at work had changed, and he was often home for dinner, but he turned the dining room table into a battleground more nights than not.

I soon noticed that two-year-old Rebecca was not eating. Some nights, she just sat quietly at the table and played with her food. Soon she was crawling down from the table and sitting on the stairs, not attempting to eat at all.

She was old enough to hear and see the daily battles Maurice threw my way.

Once a robust and jolly little girl, Rebecca grew thin and sickly. After repeated trips to the doctor, I was told she was a drama queen looking for attention and belonged on the stage. I knew that was not the problem.

Her father was the problem, and his constant yelling and screaming at me was greatly affecting her.

I made her milk shakes every day with whole milk, bananas or other fruit, and vitamins in them. She guzzled them down for a while, at least until the day she saw me make one. I guess she wasn't a fan of what I was putting in there.

The doctor assured me that as soon as she got hungry enough, she would eat. Eventually she did, but she never joined us at the table again.

Rebecca had always been very loving toward her father, but now she wouldn't get close to him, sit on his lap, or tell him she loved him. This hurt Maurice, but he had only himself to blame. Couldn't he see the damage he was doing to her?

I had little contact with Mom during this period, although she didn't live far away from us. I wanted the children to get to know their grandparents but wasn't interested in them being around the ones they had.

Mom was visibly ill and had the innocence and demeanor of a child. I tried to get her to interact with the kids, but she was unable to hold their attention for long.

Angelina made herself scarce and rarely left New England, but for some reason, she'd bonded with my mother and actually loved her. For a woman who was eaten up with bitterness and pettiness, she found a loving and caring relationship with Mom who was the only person Angelina never spoke unkindly about.

They wrote back and forth to each other, and oftentimes Mom would let me read the letters.

It was surprising to me that a woman who was so heartless to me and my daughter could convey such sweet sentiments to another person.

She even tried to convince Maurice that Rebecca and Gregory were not his. She also insisted that I raise the children Catholic, but I refused. I wanted the children to choose their own path when they were old enough.

Her reply was, "My arms will never hold a Protestant child!"

The Country Life

It was 1968. Rebecca was four years old and would be attending kindergarten in the fall of the following year.

We had heard from our neighbors that the children would be bussed to an inner-city school across town. We did not want our little girl to be bussed anywhere. Though the area we lived in was nice enough, it was a suburb of a busy city, and crime was beginning to creep into our once peaceful town.

In fact, two young girls had recently been kidnapped from the local shopping center.

Maurice and I decided it was time to look for another place to live.

He had grown up on a farm with wealthy parents who were the first people on their road to afford electricity. He had milked over 100 cows every morning before going to school, and he wanted his children to be "country" children, too. We still owned the farm in West Virginia and enjoyed taking the kids up there on weekends.

I loved being out in the country, and each time we drove down the long, dusty lane that lead to the old farmhouse, it brought back memories of me and Maurice when we first started dating.

Before we got married, we enjoyed taking road trips and often commented on the rustic houses we passed. We recalled one such place, in a little mountain area called Pleasant Valley. It was over an hour from the city and had seemed like heaven on earth back then, so we decided to make a trip out there to look around.

As we traveled the back roads, we came upon a saltbox farmhouse that had a For Sale by Owner sign in the front yard.

We stopped and met the owners, who had a house full of foster children they'd taken in over the years. I loved children, and they clamored around me, which made Rebecca extremely jealous.

The house was smaller inside than it appeared but was full of country charm and a lot of love. There was an old barn on the hill, tire swings in every tree, and even an old tree house in a sprawling cherry tree.

According to the owners, the house had been built in 1800, sixty years before the Civil War. There had been a stone fence surrounding the property at one time, but the owners had taken it down since it attracted snakes.

There had been a springhouse in the front yard where three majestic maple trees now stood. It was said that Civil War soldiers used to walk the road and stop at the springhouse to drink.

The house had also been used as a makeshift hospital during the war.

Maurice had no curiosity about such things, but I was intrigued. After finding a Civil War bullet in the driveway, I was convinced we should buy. A few months later, on July 1, 1968, we moved in and began to live our country life.

The house was old and not without its problems, but we had worked hard as a couple to purchase it, and we were proud of our new home.

The children settled in nicely and soon made friends with the neighborhood children. Life was good.

Then Jewell called. She was having more problems with Mom and asked if she could live with us. I said no, and it started an argument between us. Jewell said she had taken on the burden of caring for Mom for the past several years, and it was my turn to care for her.

I reminded her that she'd been too young to remember what Mom had put us through as children, and I had done my share of caring for them. I had practically raised her and Wade, and I was not about to raise Mom, too. Those days were over for me, and my resentment toward her grew.

Finally she had enough and sent Mom off to Ohio to live with Wade and his family. They had a small guesthouse on their property that suited her just fine. I had very little contact with Mom after that.

* * *

I had not seen Daddy since I left Kentucky when I was sixteen. Jewell had given out our phone number to just about everyone in Kentucky, and a handful of family members I didn't even know existed would call me on a regular basis. Couldn't they see I want nothing more to do with that life?

They would call and ask for me by my nickname, Sissy, and if the kids answered the phone, they didn't know who Sissy was, so they'd run and ask me. If Maurice answered, he would say, "It's your hillbilly family from Kentucky."

These people were the children my father had sired with his two other wives. I had never known them and, quite honestly, had no desire to hear about their problems. Each time they called, I thought something might have happened to Daddy, but it was never about him.

I used the calls to find out about Daddy, though, and learned he had moved to Maryland. I went to see him.

He hadn't changed much over the years. He was kind to us and showered the children with the love he had once shown me as a little girl, his honey girl. I was glad he was affectionate toward my children, but it made me long for all I'd missed over the years.

Daddy's house was surrounded by a forest of weeds as high as my shoulders and was basically a shack. When I had to go to the bathroom, he pointed down a dusty, dirt path toward a rickety lean-to. Some things never changed.

It was his birthday and very hot in June, and he had a beautiful birthday cake decorated with big yellow roses made out of buttercream. Rebecca was thrilled when he gave her the biggest one.

I didn't see him again until 1980, a few months before he died of cancer in Hurricane Creek, Kentucky. He was seventy-two.

I had not told Maurice the extent of my family woes and knew from experience that if a man knows something about you, he'll throw it up to you at some point in the relationship. What he did know about Mom was enough. I'd spent years hearing him refer to her as "that whore" and that "nut case mother of yours," and I was constantly compared to her. I was also instructed on how to raise "his" children so they would not grow up to be "insane" like my mother.

The more I defended her, the more I felt like I should not. Although those things were true about her, I didn't care to hear them. Often Rebecca would be in the other room and with her hearing, could hear the grass grow and heard them, too. Later, she would ask me, "Am I going to be crazy like Grandma when I grow up?"

I hated Maurice for putting me in a position that required me to explain such things to her. And to be honest, I had no answers myself.

At some point, Jewell went to Ohio to visit Mom, who constantly asked about me. She wrote often and although I wrote her back when I could, I made no real effort to do so.

Maybe I should have felt guilty that Wade and his family were taking care of Mom. Maybe I should have felt guilty that Jewell had cared for her for many years, but I had not. But Wade and Jewell were a lot younger and did not see the side of her I saw as a child. They had not witnessed the horrors I'd witnessed or felt the shame I'd faced on a daily basis. They could not possibly harbor the same resentment toward Mom, so why should I feel guilty?

I was married and had two young children with my husband and a teenager with Grant. I had a lovely farmhouse on twenty-seven acres and owned another large farm in West Virginia. I was somebody now—not a nobody, like I grew up thinking I would be.

I hadn't married some hillbilly with a bottle full of pee for a proposal or a drunk destined to get himself killed on the railroad tracks. I had not been a young widow with a dead husband whose lungs were full of coal dust, and I was no longer the daughter of the town whore.

Let that title go to Jewell, who chose to stay behind and rot with the rest of them.

Why did they all have to follow me everywhere I went? Was I the leader of the pack? Did I have all the answers and just didn't know it?

The Diagnosis

I wanted to live in peace with my husband and my children. Why wouldn't the past leave me alone and stay buried? I wanted Mom to disappear and take her mental problems with her.

Then I got the call from Jewell.

While Jewell was in Ohio, Mom begged to go back to Maryland with her and Jewell agreed. She only wanted to visit her "other daughter and her young'uns" and promised she wouldn't stay long.

While she was here, Jewell noticed a large, hard-looking lump on her collarbone.

Mom was on welfare and could not afford proper medical care, but Jewell took her to the local hospital anyway. She said the doctor was foreign, and she couldn't understand what he was telling her, which wasn't much. After the testing, she broke away from Mom and ran after him.

"Doctor, does my mother have cancer? I need to know."

He calmly said, "Oh yes."

Jewell felt it was not a good idea to tell her, but I disagreed. No matter what type of relationship we'd had with Mom, she had a right to know.

Well, Jewell told her she was fine, and she was taken back to Wade's, though Jewell informed him of the diagnosis. Sadly, he and his wife agreed that Mom should not be told she was terminally ill. Again, I fought them on this.

A few weeks after her return to Ohio, Mom

was admitted to the hospital for surgery to remove her cancerous right lung and collarbone.

I went to Ohio to be with her. I walked into the room, and there she was, asleep on the bed, her skin still as flawless as a porcelain doll. Her long, wavy, auburn hair had been cut short because it was too painful to raise her arm to care for it.

Mom had been diagnosed with cancer of the chest cavity and at fifty-seven years old, given only a year to live.

The nurse walked in and informed me that Mom was not asleep but in a light coma she had fallen into after her surgery.

I was the only one at the hospital, having told Wade and his wife I would be there for her after she came back into her room. They planned on visiting later that night after work.

I asked the nurse if Mom could hear me, and she said she had no way of knowing, but if I wanted to talk to her, I could. I went to her bedside and gently took her hand. It was as soft and supple as a woman half her age.

I calmly stroked her hand and stared at her. She was breathtaking, and I could see right then and there how Daddy had fallen in love with her. I could also see why every man in town wanted to be with her and why every woman was envious of her and her charms.

Hell, I was envious of her at that moment! Although I had grown into a fine-looking woman myself, nothing compared to the beauty of the woman that lay in that bed before me.

"What happened to us?" I thought. "What

happened to you, Mom, to make you so different? To make you not love us anymore?"

I hadn't realized I was talking out loud until I looked up at her and watched a single tear slide slowly down her cheek.

After several days in a coma, she awoke to find me, Wade, and Jewell in her room. All her kids, but one, Opal, were there for her.

She kept asking what was wrong with her, and the others assured her she was going to be fine and live a long and healthy life. I was sickened by their lies. For God's sake, someone needed to tell her the truth!

The others left just before visiting hours were over, and I sat down on the bed next to her.

"How you feeling, Mom? You okay?"

"Well, I would sure like to get out of this place and go home," she said as she shifted uncomfortably in her bed.

I didn't know if she meant home to Wade's or back to Kentucky, but I didn't ask; it didn't matter.

"Virgie?" she said, her eyes sad and tired. "Tell me the truth, baby. Is something wrong with me?"

I realized then that she had never lost her sweet honey accent. It reminded me of long ago, before she left us, when she'd read bedtime stories to us. I also remembered a promised we'd made to each other when I was just a kid: if either of us knew the other was terminally ill, we would tell them.

I didn't think she'd made that promise with the other children, so I was bound to do the right thing.

I sighed, swallowed hard and said, "Yes, Mom, you have cancer."

She looked at me as though I'd slapped her in the face. I waited for her reaction; it came slowly.

Her eyes welled with tears. "Well, how bad is it? Is that what this purple thing on my neck is?"

I explained to her the type of cancer she had and that it was inoperable. She didn't know what that meant, and when I told her she began to cry.

"Well, you mean they can't get this thing out of me? Is that what you're telling me, Virgie?"

Swallowing back tears, I said, "Yes."

We cried together for a few moments and then she whispered, "How long they sayin' I got?"

"About a year."

I stayed a while longer, and before I left, she called me to her bedside.

"Thank you, baby, for telling me. Now I can tell some people things I've been wantin' to tell 'em and tell some other people some things I ought not to tell 'em, but they gotta be said."

I smiled. I knew exactly what she meant.

I had to get back to Maryland, so I told Mom good-bye. I told her I'd see her soon, but we both knew I might not make it back up to Ohio before . . . you know.

It was a nine-hour drive, and I cried all the

way home. I'd no sooner gotten into the house when the phone rang. It was Jewell.

"How could you tell Mom she had cancer? We all agreed not to tell her! Do you know what that will do to her?"

I sighed. "Jewell, look, I never agreed not to tell her, and she had every right to know. How dare you and Wade keep something like that from her? She has a right to get her affairs in order and to make amends or just tell people good-bye. Don't you understand that?"

After a few more angry words from my little sister, she hung up on me.

As soon as the phone hit the cradle, it rang again. It was Betty, Wade's wife.

"I cannot believe you waited until we all left your mother's hospital room, and then you sneak back in there and tell her she has cancer. We promised each other not to tell her!"

Another heavy sigh. "Betty, I just got off the phone with Jewell. I made no such promise to any of you, but I did make one to Mom when I was a kid. She made me promise I would tell her if she was ever terminally ill, and I asked her to do the same for me. She had a right to know!"

"Well, your brother is not too happy with you, either. You know, we're the ones taking care of her and feeding her and paying her bills. We have the right to make the decisions concerning her care. What are you and Maurice doing to help her?"

I was not going to get into it with her. I liked Betty, and we had all grown up together in Pikeville, but she did not know what took place inside our family.

"As for Mom's bills," I said, "she's on medical assistance, and the two of you are not paying anything out of pocket for her. Nothing! Yes, you're giving her a place to live and feeding her, but you offered to take her in. Now, I just got home after driving nine hours. I'm hot, tired, hungry, and the kids and Maurice are hungry, so I'm hanging up. Goodnight."

She hung up on me first.

A few months later, Wade called and said Mom wanted to speak to me. She asked if she could come down for a visit and see the young'uns one more time, and of course I said yes. Wade got back on the phone, and there was no mention of the argument between me and Betty. He offered to bring her down to visit if we could drive her back to Ohio.

When they arrived, Mom was frail and thin but still lovely, and I knew this would be the last time we'd see her. She stayed with us for two weeks and even got daily phone calls from Angelina, who was secretly heartbroken at the thought of losing one of the few people in the world who actually enjoyed talking to her.

It felt strange to have Mom in the house with us, although she was so quiet and gentle it was like having a kitten for a houseguest.

She wore an oversized white smock for most of her visit and constantly kept her hand down the top of her blouse.

When I asked her why she did that, she

removed her hand to expose a large, eggplant-looking tumor that had nestled itself onto her collarbone. I recoiled in shock.

Then I noticed the look of shame on her face, as though having cancer was somehow her fault, and I was embarrassed by my reaction.

While training to be a nurse back in Kentucky, I'd seen everything from dead babies to diseased whores, but I had never seen anything so grotesque as that tumor.

I wondered why it couldn't be removed. Was she destined to walk the rest of her days with it attached to her neck? Was it a punishment of some sort? Was it a badge of honor or a scarlet letter of adultery?

I found out later that the roots of the tumor had grown too deep into her surrounding tissues, and the word *inoperable* meant just that.

I was even more surprised when I learned she had taken up smoking. She said she'd always wondered what all the fuss was about, so she decided to try it.

This outraged the family, who said smoking cigarettes was bad for her and would kill her.

Did they not realize how ridiculous they sounded? I encouraged her, telling her to try anything she wanted. What did it matter now?

I packed Mom up, and Maurice, the kids, and I made the long trip to Cincinnati to take her back to Wade's. We spent the night before heading out the next morning.

It was a bittersweet good-bye, as I knew I'd never see Mom alive again. I cried as we left Ohio, and Maurice, like a vulture smelling blood and weakness, pounced on me.

"Why are you crying over her? You don't even like the woman."

"She's still my mother, for God's sake!" I cried.

It was a silent nine-hour drive back to Maryland.

* * *

Months passed and I got weekly updates as to Mom's condition. Jewell and Donald had divorced, which left her time to make trips to see Mom. Eve was now a wayward child who rebelled against her mother and her church.

Jewell had become a devout Mormon and immersed herself in the lifestyle; in turn, Eve rebelled.

As a kid growing up in the 60s, the last thing she wanted was to be told she was not allowed to do something, like wear clothing that revealed her arms or drink tea and coffee.

Even as a child, she and Jewell got into horrible shouting matches. One such argument occurred because Eve said Jesus had long hair, and Jewell insisted he did not.

Unknown to me at the time, Eve was being physically abused by Jewell, who denied all accusations. If I had known, I would have taken Eve from her and raised her myself.

Eve was extremely close to her father, and the split was difficult on her. I was not surprised to hear of the divorce, only surprised that he had not killed her during the marriage.

Donald moved into an apartment with his mother, who later found him dead in his bedroom. He had died from a bleeding ulcer brought on by alcohol poisoning.

Our children were now three and four and living the country life.

Their days revolved around mud pies, Barbie dolls, GI Joes and tire swings. We had chickens, ducks, goats, rabbits, cats, dogs, two cows, and even a pony named Candy.

It was an idyllic childhood, and I was grateful we were able to provide them with such a life.

I'd made a vow long ago that I would never, ever allow my children to grow up like I had. I could have turned into a bitter, angry woman, but I chose to be happy. I had a lot of love to give and lavished my children with affection every day.

I even found myself quoting Mom on occasion. When I hugged the kids goodnight, I'd ask them how much they loved me, and I taught them to say, "I love you with a bushel and a peck and a hug around the neck."

I remembered a lot of the good times with Mom before she was different. She had been a good woman, a decent wife and mother before she turned to other men and prostitution.

No matter who was at fault during those painful times, I blamed her.

A mother is supposed to be there for her children, to protect them and keep them safe from harm and evil, to love them no matter what.

But that was not the case.

The Funeral

A few months after Mom got back to Ohio, I got a call from Wade. Mom had died in her sleep the night before, and they'd found her that morning. She'd been given a year to live and died eleven months and twenty-nine days after her diagnosis.

Wade, Betty, and Jewell blamed me, saying she would have lived longer if I had not told her how long the doctor had predicted her to live.

A funeral was planned for the following week, and I offered to send money to help with expenses.

I was feeling a mixture of emotions, and I tried to detach myself and act as though it was a stranger who had died instead of my mother. In reality, she had been a stranger to me and to her other children.

We didn't know who she was when she came home from the hospital and she didn't know us. We were just a bunch of people she was told was her family. She had no choice but to believe it, but she couldn't make it stick.

After Wade and I got off the phone, I knew I had to tell Maurice, but I hated to. Only months before, he had made the trip to Ohio with me to take Mom back to Wade's. Now he would have to make the trip again, and I knew he'd be unhappy.

I knew how Maurice felt about Mom, although he never got a chance to really know her. He had only heard stories about her, and they were never pleasant to hear. I don't even know why I told him. I guess somewhere deep down inside I wanted to confide in someone, someone who wasn't from the hills or from my ever-growing family, someone who would understand.

But he didn't understand. He cast scorn and ridicule in my face and even disapproved when I went without shoes, calling me a hillbilly.

At times I felt as though he wanted to turn the children against me. Rebecca was not only his spitting image, but she was developing his personality as well.

She would not go barefoot in the summertime like the other children because "Daddy said only hillbillies walk around without their shoes."

I hoped that when the children were old enough, they would know my past, learn from it, and never want to repeat it.

I did everything I could to be different from my mother, to protect my children from evil men and dishonest women. I hoped I'd made a difference in their lives.

Surprisingly, he didn't react the way I expected. He calmly asked me when the funeral was and how much money Wade needed. I told him I had some money set aside for this, but he insisted on giving me money to send. I took it and thanked him.

Jewell called and asked if she could ride to Ohio with us. We didn't have room in the car for her and Eve, so she reluctantly said she would take the train.

The drive was long and quiet. The children played in the backseat, and I tried to occupy them with car games like I Spy, but after a while, I too was bored with the drive.

I wondered if anyone had called Daddy. I didn't even know where he was, though I assumed he went back to Kentucky.

He and Laverne had divorced and after having a total of fourteen children between Mom, Jenny, and Laverne, I hoped he was taking a break from marriage and birthing children and was living alone. I also hoped he was okay.

I felt a profound sense of sadness as we pulled into Wade's narrow driveway. Out back, I could see the guesthouse where Mom had lived and died. She had spent her last moments in that tiny, wooden house. My mind raced with unanswered questions: Who found her? What did she look like? Was she in pain at the end? Had she still been using her cloth napkins from Tarragon?

Wade's house was full of people. He, Betty, their four children and two dogs were all sitting in the living room when we arrived.

I was always impressed with the fact that his dogs were so well trained that they never crossed the line into any other room unless he gave them permission to do so.

Maybe it was because Wade had not been home from Vietnam long. We were all terrified when he left and prayed for his safe return. Like most soldiers who have seen the horrors of war, he did not discuss them.

I don't know if he talked to Betty about it in

private, but knowing my brother, he did not.

He had grown into a very handsome man with a keen sense of humor, dimples and a cleft chin. He was often quiet but quick witted and after all these years, I still called him Jug.

Wade had confided in me that he'd met a woman over there who was not only his friend during the war, but his lover. He felt a great deal of love for her, and at some point I felt bad for his wife.

But unknown to Betty, he'd had another woman in Kentucky who bore him a son Betty never knew about.

I would have been suspicious if my husband insisted on taking separate vacations to Kentucky every few months and did not see fit to include me. Either she was none the wiser or accepted that way of life. I don't know.

Wade had his children trained as well. He kept the television so low that it was almost impossible to hear. For someone like me who was deaf in one ear, it was completely inaudible.

Suddenly, a flood of memories came rushing back to haunt me. I was eight years old and had wondered off into the woods by myself. I had so much stress and tension at home; I used to go off and hide just to be alone sometime.

I was a curious child with the fearlessness of a warrior, and I would seek adventure at every turn.

I came across a huge tree and saw a gray, papery cocoon hanging from a low branch above my head. I saw a bee or two buzzing around, but never thought much of it.

Curious about what was inside, I stuck a stick as far inside the cocoon as it would go and swirled it around.

Within seconds, I was covered in hornets. They attacked the left side of my face with a vengeance. I screamed but thought I was too far away for anyone to hear me. The pain was intense as hundreds of hornets stung me. I felt my head swelling, and I couldn't open my left eye.

I guess I passed out, because I awoke in my own bed surrounded by Mom, Daddy, our neighbor, Jack, and some other people I didn't know.

I couldn't see out of my left eye or hear out of my left ear. I had cold compresses and mud stuck to the side of my face, and I could taste vomit in my mouth.

I heard Daddy say, "Jack, it's a good thing you found her. She would have died out there."

"Well, Jess, I heard the screams, and when I saw it was Virgie, I brought her here."

He'd been out in the woods making moonshine, and I came close to stumbling upon his still. He said the bees kept a lot of nosy people away.

I laid in bed for over a week. The swelling in my eye had gone down, but the hearing in my left ear never returned.

I thought it was just as well. I had heard enough on that side of life anyway.

Due to Maurice's work schedule, we were only able to attend the funeral, having missed the viewing the night before.

Wade suggested we stay with them, and we felt like we were putting them out since they had a house full of kids already. He was used to company and said the three boys could sleep on the sofa bed in the living room, their young daughter could sleep with them, and the four of us could take the remaining two bedrooms. So Gregory and Maurice took one room, and Rebecca and I took the other.

I had never really gotten to see Wade and Betty interact as a married couple, and I found them endearing.

After they married in Pikeville, they moved across the Ohio River and settled into the home they now occupied. I had known her as a little girl, and she still carried with her that sweet Kentucky twang and doted on Wade like a king.

Wade's house sat between other houses on a side street away from town. It was a comfortable house with a nice back yard and deck overlooking the patio and grill.

They were always cooking out and inviting people to their home, and I almost envied the fact that they enjoyed themselves.

In fact, being with them brought back many memories.

Maurice, the kids, and I lived a sheltered life when we first moved to the country; I was isolated and alone. I made friends with several of the women on our road but found they reminded me a great deal of the women I'd left behind in Kentucky. Gossips, rumor mills, secret affairs, and troubled marriages lurked all around me.

It's true that no matter where you go, you take your troubles with you; people are the same everywhere.

The grass may be greener on the other side, but you still have to mow your lawn.

Maurice was a good father, but he felt he owned us, and we shouldn't need anyone but each other. I had grown up with an open-door lifestyle—people coming and going in the house, relatives visiting, traveling salesmen sleeping over—and although it was a hard life, it was an open and honest one.

With Maurice, all that changed. We'd had our share of cocktail parties and the Washington nightlife before we settled down, so when we had children, we were ready and truly wanted them.

But moving so far out in the country, away from everyone, made me long for a friend other than my husband and my children.

I had no desire to go out with friends to clubs or social mixers, but I'd hoped to be able to invite people to our home. I did on occasion, and Maurice did not like it. He was cordial to them, but as soon as they left, he yelled at me for having someone else in "his" home.

I was proud of Maurice for behaving so kindly during this stressful time in my family. He managed to be nice to everyone, though he referred to my brother as weak.

He told me he thought of him that way when he first came home from the war. They were shooting guns at the farm, and Wade made a casual comment about killing himself.

I never knew the whole story, but who knows what demons were deep inside Wade after spending time in Vietnam? Maurice had no right to judge him. He had not seen action during war time.

At times, living with Maurice was like being in a war zone in Vietnam. I often felt I was walking through a field of land mines, never knowing when I was going to take a wrong step, trip the bomb, and set of an explosive fight.

I had to step lightly at all times. I was grateful that he had managed his temper while were there but did not look forward to the long ride home.

I used to say, "a fight a day keeps the psychiatrist away," but in my heart, I hated living that way.

I had to tuck my memories away and move forward.

The morning of the funeral came, and I woke up slowly. During my slumber, I had momentarily forgotten that Mom had just died and upon remembering, felt sick to my stomach.

I loved her as my mother, but I hated her as my Mom.

I was shamed by her and ashamed *of* her. I would forever be the daughter of the town whore, and I would never be able to wash that stain away.

I got the kids up and ready and could smell coffee coming from the kitchen. Betty, in her normal routine of taking care of my brother and their children, was up and making breakfast.

Wade had his own heating and air conditioning business in town, and Betty worked for him. He had to go into the office for an hour that morning but assured us he would be home to attend the service together.

Maurice was not a man who ate breakfast but survived on a few cups of coffee in the morning, and Betty was quick to oblige. I watched as she doted on him and realized how much she needed to be needed.

Their older kids were just waking up, and Rebecca and Gregory were told to grab a plate and sit at the table. Rebecca still didn't eat like everyone else, and Betty made sure she had the type of cereal she liked.

I took a sip of coffee and added a little more sugar to the cup.

"Has anyone called Daddy?" I asked Betty as I took a seat at the table.

Flipping a stack of pancakes onto a plate, she said, "I don't know if Jesse knows or not. Wade didn't say anything. You know how he is."

Yes, I did indeed know how he was.

I loved Jug and recalled all the times I took his little chubby hand and told him things would be all right. I had no idea if they would be or not, but I was his big sister. I had to make sure he was not afraid.

When we were little, we'd go walking in the woods, and the sky would grow dark. Although we never really lost our way, the fear was there that we might.

Wade would start whistling, and I never questioned him about it until we were older.

"I was afraid all the time," he said. "Whistling took my mind off the fear."

It was almost ten o'clock, and Wade was just pulling into the driveway. I could hear him whistling from inside the house.

I wondered how much he remembered from our childhood. He was so young when most of the horrors occurred however I am sure he remembered being in foster care. Anytime I ever tried to bring it up, he would say, "Well Sissy, that was a long time ago."

When he come inside, Wade surprised me by asking Maurice to come outside to see his new boat. He did so, though Maurice was not an outdoorsman in any way, shape, or form. He didn't hunt or seek adventure. The only outdoor thing I ever saw him do was ride the tractor to mow the grass, which sent him into a sneezing spell due to his hay fever. I think, too, that he only pretended to like Wade . . . but with him, it was hard to tell

I felt a slight headache coming on and told Betty I wanted to lie back down for a few minutes until it was time to leave. She assured me that we had plenty of time since the church was only a few minutes away.

I went back into the bedroom and lay down on the cool, cotton sheets of the unmade bed. The red velvet spread had been pulled back to reveal the crisp clean cotton. My head throbbed, and as I rested on the soft, down pillow, I could feel myself drift off into a deep, comforting sleep.

* * *

I turned away from the droning sound of Aunt Frances's voice as she went on and on about Mom. Didn't she realize I had heard enough? I stood up and walked away from her.

I approached my mother for the last time and gazed at the beautiful, still woman in the casket before me. I knew we would never be that physically close again.

I gently took her hand and placed it in mine. The bitter coldness did not match the radiant glow that surrounded her like a halo. Even in death, she breathed life.

I tilted my head to look down into her face. I studied every nonexistent line and wrinkle and the creases in her lips that were stained with her favorite shade of Tangee lipstick.

I thought of all the men besides Daddy who had kissed those lips and touched her willowy body—the body that bore five children yet could still wear my brother's size-four belt.

Her fingers slipped inside mine, and I twisted the ring on her left hand. It was the tiny wedding ring she got from Daddy to replace the one she'd mysteriously lost. I never told her I'd taken her original one and buried it, since I felt she didn't deserve it.

I caressed the wavy, auburn hair around her dainty ears and thought of how many times those ears had heard harsh words from me: I hate you; I wish you were dead; Whore!

I thought of how I'd made her life a living hell to punish her for making mine the same. I'd punished her all this time, blamed her, hated her, only to find it was not her fault.

Why didn't someone tell me the truth?

"I'm sorry, Mom," I whispered as I walked away, finally letting her rest in peace.

The End

About the Author

Lisa V. Proulx is the bestselling author of several books.

She lives in her childhood home in Maryland, has raised Rottweilers for over 15 years and is an inspirational speaker.

www.lisavproulx.com

32388007R00162

Made in the USA
Middletown, DE
02 June 2016